ABORTION

Abortion

FACING THE ISSUES

SUSAN
NEIBURG
TERKEL

*Franklin Watts/1988/An Impact Book
New York/London/Toronto/Sydney*

Library of Congress Cataloging-in-Publication Data

Terkel, Susan Neiburg.
Abortion/Susan Neiburg Terkel.
p.   cm.—(An Impact book)
Bibliography: p.
Includes index.
Summary: Examines the history, legal status, ethics, politics, and medicla aspects of abortion and uses personal accounts of women who have had abortions to illuminate both sides of the issue.
ISBN 0-531-10565-2
1. Abortion—United States. 2. Abortion—United States—Moral and ethical aspects. 3. Abortion—Law and legislation—United States.
[1. Abortion.] I. Title.
HQ767.5.U5T47 1988
363.4'6'0973—dc19   88-14228 CIP AC

Copyright © 1988 by Susan Neiburg Terkel
All rights reserved
Printed in the United States of America
6 5 4 3 2 1

*This book is dedicated to my parents,
Deborah and Sidney Neiburg*

Illustration on p. 45
by Anne Canevari Green

Diagrams by Vantage Art

Sources for charts: Religious Coalition for Abortion Rights, p. 47; National Abortion Federation, pp. 59, 83; Alan Guttmacher Institute, pp. 73, 75, 78 (left); Center for Disease Control, p. 78 (left); Raymond Adamek, "Abortion and Public Opinion in the United States," National Right to Life Educational Trust Fund, 1986.

Photographs courtesy of:
AP/Wide World Photos: pp. 15, 39, 94, 106;
Photo Researchers, Inc.: pp. 49, 61 (both Erika Stone, Eastern Women's Center), 124 (J. Stevenson/Science Photo Library); Laima E. Druskis: pp. 101, 104, 114.

CONTENTS

Preface 11

Chapter 1
Legalizing Abortion
13

Chapter 2
Roe v. *Wade*
29

Chapter 3
How Abortions Are Performed
43

Chapter 4
The Abortion Industry
57

Chapter 5
Women Who Obtain Abortions
69

Chapter 6
The Way People Feel about Abortion
81

Chapter 7
The Politics of Abortion
93

Chapter 8
Why Women Have Abortions
111

Chapter 9
The Ethical Issue
121

Source Notes 139

Bibliography 143

For Further Reading 153

Index 155

Special gratitude to my editor, Iris Rosoff, who offered objective, but kind advice; to my agent, Andrea Brown, for encouraging me to write about abortion; to my consultants, Margaret Pepe, Ph.D., and Mary Mahowald, Ph.D., for helping me to clarify my thoughts on abortion and understand the issue from each point of view; and to my assistant, Kathy Moran, for her astute observations and research.

Further thanks to Ed Markovich and Raymond J. Adamek and Akron Right to Life Committee; Pamela Morgan and the Boston Women's Health Collective; Vicky Jaffe and Emily Tynes and National Abortion Rights Action League; Diana Traub and the Reproduction Freedom Project of the American Civil Liberties Union; Susan Tew and the Alan Guttmacher Institute; Eileen Roberts and Cleveland American Civil Liberties Union; Gina Oberndorf and Fredrica F. Hodges and the Religious Coalition for Abortion Rights; Alice Kirkman and the National Abortion Federation; and Stephanie Johnson from Senator Gordon Humphrey's office.

Appreciation also goes to Thomas Schneider, Rev. Philip J. Boyle, Ronalee Cargould, Scott Blumberg, the Hudson Library, and most of all to my husband, Lawrence Terkel, for keeping the family together while I burned the midnight oil completing this book.

PREFACE

What is interesting about not writing an objective, dispassionate book about abortion, but instead trying to write an objective, *passionate* book about abortion is that depending on the conviction of the reader, I am constantly accused of being partial to the "other side." Thus, those in sympathy with pro-life have accused me of being partial to pro-choice, and those in sympathy with pro-choice have accused me of being partial to pro-life. What this criticism has shown me is that perhaps I have been successful in being passionate about each point of view. For throughout the writing of this manuscript, I have tried to consider not only the logical and persuasive arguments representatives of each viewpoint have put forth, but also the poignantly written letters I read. These letters were written by women whose lives were deeply affected by abortion, both legal and illegal, and who were pro-life or pro-choice because of their experience. It is their voices, I believe, that give the book its passion, and it was listening to their tales that gave me the ability to be sympathetic to both sides of the issue, rather than to be coldly objective.

Chapter One

LEGALIZING ABORTION

Today abortions are legal, available, and, for the vast majority of women obtaining them, medically safe. Yet less than twenty-five years ago, the prospects for a safe, legal abortion were slim.

Consider the case of Norma McCorvey from Texas. It is August 1969. Ms. McCorvey is divorced, poor, and a single parent. She is supporting herself and a daughter by working as a waitress. She is pregnant and feels she cannot support another child. Ms. McCorvey is told by her doctor that she cannot have an abortion in Texas because, according to the state law, abortion is legal only if her life is in danger, which it is not. Unable to have a legal abortion in Texas, unable to afford to go to California, where abortions are legal, unable to afford an illegal abortion anywhere, depressed and bitter, Ms. McCorvey decides to lie about her circumstances, making up a story about being raped by four people.[1] Why did Norma McCorvey lie? Perhaps she did this hoping that a story about being raped might somehow overcome the state law, or perhaps she did this for more sympathy for her predicament. She may even have done this to conceal the actual circumstances of being an unwed mother, because in 1969, women were often disparaged for being pregnant outside of marriage.

Although Ms. McCorvey has the option of keeping her baby, she decides in the best interests of herself, her daughter, and the future of the baby, to place the baby for adoption. The first lawyer she approaches for help with the adoption asks her "rude" questions about her rape. "I just didn't like his attitude," said Ms. McCorvey later in an interview, "so on a whim, I got another lawyer." This new lawyer introduces her to two recent graduates of the University of Texas Law School: Sarah Weddington and Linda Coffee. They persuade Ms. McCorvey to take her case to court and to challenge the Texas statute that denied her a legal abortion. She agrees.

In June of the following year, Ms. McCorvey gives birth to a baby girl. In order not to become emotionally attached to her baby, Ms. McCorvey has requested that the nurses not bring the baby in to her. Unfortunately, one of the nurses is unaware of the woman's request and brings her the child. As soon as another nurse realizes what is happening, she rushes to Ms. McCorvey's room and quickly returns the baby to the hospital nursery.

Norma McCorvey, the Dallas, Texas mother whose desire to have an abortion was the basis for the landmark Supreme Court decision in 1973 legalizing abortion. Although she originally claimed to have been raped, in 1987 she retracted her story and said she had lied.

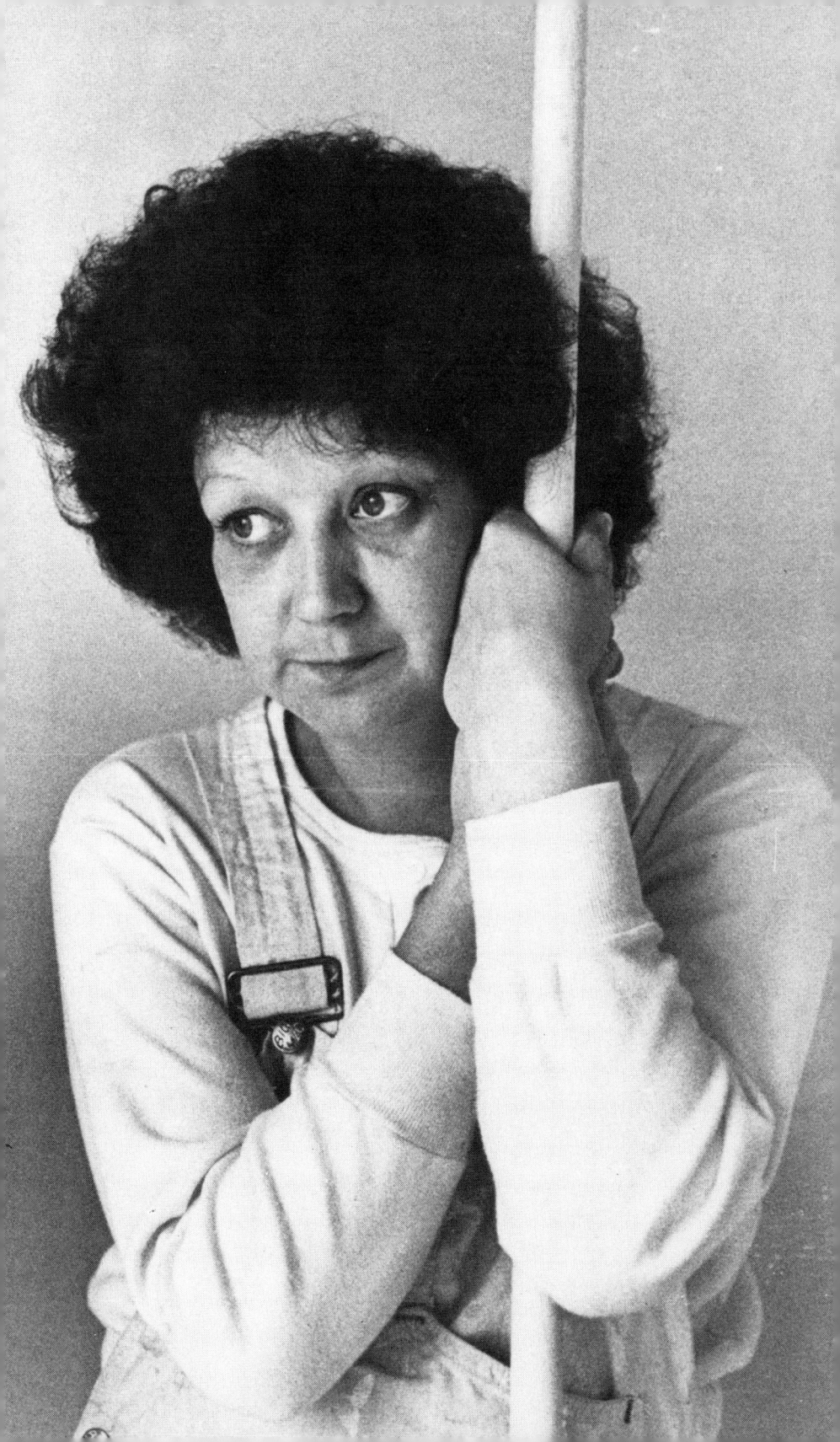

With the legal assistance of her two lawyers and several large organizations that were trying to legalize abortion through the judicial system, Ms. McCorvey files a class action suit against Henry Wade, the District Attorney in Dallas, Texas. She uses the pseudonym, "Jane Roe," to protect her identity. The case, *Roe* v. *Wade,* eventually goes to the Supreme Court, where along with another case—*Doe* v. *Bolton*—it becomes the pivotal Supreme Court decision that legalized abortion.

THE FIRST ABORTION LAWS

Prior to *Roe* v. *Wade,* each state had its own abortion statutes (laws) prescribing when an abortion in that state was legal and when it was illegal. Sometimes the current debate on abortion makes it seem as though abortion had been illegal forever before the Supreme Court ruling in 1973. But, in fact, it is only within the last two hundred years that abortion was even a legal rather than a personal decision.

Our abortion laws come from Anglo-Saxon tradition.[2] The first two cases, back in 1327 and 1348 respectively, established the common-law right to terminate a pregnancy at any time. The *Twinslayer's Case* involved a woman pregnant with twins who was beaten so severely she miscarried, and her twins died. The man who had beaten her was indicted for murder, pleaded not guilty, and was released because the judges refused to call the crime a murder. In the second case, the *Abortionist's Case,* a man was indicted for murder for actually inducing an abortion. He was acquitted on the grounds that it could not be proven whether the fetus had died from the abortion or from a natural cause shortly before the abortion, and also on grounds that the fetus had no baptismal name. This lack of proof of how the fetus actually died and lack of a baptismal name were the reasons why abortion was not a crime.

Abortion remained a private decision for centuries. In 1670 an English judge, Sir Matthew Hale, ruled that if a woman died as a result of an abortion, the abortionist was guilty of murder. If she did not die, the abortion was legal.

Then in 1803, the first restrictive abortion statute was passed in England: Called the Lord Ellenborough Act, it made it a crime to have an abortion after quickening, which is the moment during pregnancy when the woman first feels her fetus moving, a confirmation that she is indeed pregnant. (Until the twentieth century, there were no reliable pregnancy tests.) This law justified making abortion illegal on the grounds of protecting a woman's life and not protecting the life of the "embryo human being." For in those days, a woman's life was in danger because of the highly toxic drugs that were frequently used to induce abortion.

NINETEENTH CENTURY REFORM

At the time the Constitution was framed, abortion was a private issue and thus was never mentioned. In 1812, the first abortion case, *Commonwealth* v. *Bangs,* was heard by the Massachusetts Supreme Court, which ruled that abortion with the woman's consent was legal before quickening.

Despite the serious threat to a woman's health that abortion posed in the nineteenth century, many women used it as a primary form of birth control. Upon publication of *Fruits of Philosophy,* a classic birth control text written by Dr. Charles Knowlton (who was, incidentally, the first American to be imprisoned for advocating birth control), the birth control movement gained ground in America. Despite the development of the diaphragm in the 1840s, abortion was still used, although it was often under the guise of "menstrual regulation," since fertilization and the beginning of pregnancy were still undiscovered. Abortions, though not rare, were exceedingly dangerous. As mentioned previously, dangerous substances or practices were used either to treat "menstrual blockage" or to terminate a pregnancy. These practices ranged from bloodletting and hot baths to ingestion of poisonous substances or surgery, which was often a fatal procedure.

During the first half of the nineteenth century, a great part of the medical profession was in the hands of untrained people: some of them were lay healers and folk doctors, others charlatans and quacks. The physicians who had received their medical training from established universities were concerned about the inferior medical treatment the laypersons offered, and in particular, the abortions that the lay healers were administering. The physicians were eager to limit the practice of medicine and especially the performing of abortions to only those physicians who had earned a university medical degree. To upgrade the profession, the American Medical Association (AMA) was founded in 1847.

In 1859, the AMA passed a resolution that condemned abortion and urged state legislatures to make it illegal. In time, most of the members of the AMA supported the resolution; many lobbied in the state legislatures for a change in the abortion laws. Gradually, each of the states changed its laws, and before the end of the century, abortion was a major crime in every state. All but four states allowed therapeutic abortions only as a life-saving measure, and in those four states, even life-saving abortions were considered a crime.

BIRTH CONTROL MOVEMENT

The nineteenth century witnessed not only a crusade to change the legal status of abortion but also a crusade to introduce birth control to the American public. Much controversy surrounded the issue, and in 1873, the Comstock Law, the first federal attempt to make reproduction a public policy, was passed. Basically, the Comstock Law banned the mailing of any material considered obscene, including contraception and abortifacients (drugs that induce abortion).

Despite the federal restrictions on birth control, women, particularly those of the middle and upper class, had access to birth control; thus they were not as dependent on abortion as they once were. Though the abortion rate decreased overall, thousands of women still obtained them. An illegal abortion industry flourished, and abortion remained one of the leading causes of maternal death. In addition to the fatalities, hundreds of thousands of women suffered complications from abortions.

TWENTIETH CENTURY REPEAL

During the twentieth century, physicians were gradually beginning to change their perspective on abortion. Several factors contributed to this change. To begin with, the public grew more tolerant of birth control and also more fearful of overpopulation, especially among poor women. Also, where the United States had once been a largely rural nation, depending on large families as a source of labor, it was now an industrialized nation, in which the smaller family was desired. In addition, the medical community was concerned about the thousands of women suffering complications or death from illegal abortions at a time when legal abortions were now safer than ever due to the advent of antiseptic surgery, antibiotics, and new abortion techniques. Thus, by the middle of the century, there was a mounting campaign to liberalize the existing state abortion statutes, many of which had been law for over a century.

At the same time though, physicians were learning

more about fertilization, fetal development, and the management of safer pregnancy and delivery, reducing the need for therapeutic abortions. For many, particularly Catholic physicians, this confirmed the belief that life begins at conception. The moral issue of abortion took on new dimensions, even though Catholic theologians had condemned it for centuries (and in 1869, Pope Pius IX forbade all abortions). Theologians now entered the public arena of the abortion issue.

By the middle of this century, there was a mounting crusade to reverse the state abortion statutes, many of which had been in existence for over a century. The position of many physicians on abortion was becoming more liberal than the existing statutes reflected, and there was a mounting campaign within the American Medical Association to persuade legislatures to liberalize the state abortion laws.

The reasons for wanting to liberalize the laws varied. Some of the doctors were disturbed about laws that restricted them from performing the number of therapeutic abortions they believed needed to be performed. Although life-saving abortions remained legal in most states, hospitals nevertheless restricted the number that could be performed each month. If a hospital's quota was filled, it was difficult for a physician to extend the quota, even if a woman needed a therapeutic abortion.

In addition, there were doctors who were willing to do abortions for reasons they considered valid, but which were not included in the abortion laws. Reasons such as ending a pregnancy that was a result of rape or incest, or pregnancies that were not a threat to a woman's life but were nonetheless a threat to her physical or emotional health were considered justifiable. The laws also did not allow a physician to perform an abortion on a woman carrying a deformed fetus. Some physicians believed women were morally entitled to abortions no matter what the reason, but there were still others who performed abortions simply because it was lucrative to do so. Regardless of the motive for performing an abortion, a physician caught performing one risked losing his license and receiving a stiff jail sentence if convicted.

In 1957, responding to these physicians' desire to legalize the abortions they were already performing, the American Law Institute suggested to the state legislatures that they liberalize existing abortion statutes. This suggestion was written in the form of a proposal called the Moral Penal Code. What the ALI recommended was that the criteria for legal abortion be extended to include the mental health of the mother, pregnancy due to rape or incest, and fetal deformity: the same criteria that many physicians were already using, albeit illegally.

Not a single state legislature accepted the Moral Penal Code's suggestions. Laws change slowly, especially when the change requires going against a long tradition. Support for a law erodes when hundreds of thousands of people begin ignoring the law, and also when there is a change in the societal attitudes that first prompted the law to be enacted. When this happens, reformers usually emerge on the scene and try changing the old law to reflect the newer attitudes and the popular consensus.

If the prevailing attitude, however, infringes on the rights of minorities, a law cannot be changed. In a democracy, which seeks to protect minorities from the tyranny of the majority, the judicial system is designed in a way to be politically neutral and immune from the whims of politicians or the shifts in popular opinion. In reality, the courts do reflect shifting attitudes, only they reflect them very slowly. By the 1960s, there was a shift in the attitude toward abortion. The criteria for abortion that the Model Penal Code had proposed, though not as liberal as abortion on demand, were accepted by the majority of Americans who were polled during those years. They remain the mainstream consensus on abortion.

Sometimes one or two well-publicized incidents focus attention on laws that might need revision. For example, the assassination of a beloved public figure might focus public awareness on the need to revise gun control laws, or a mining accident might focus on the need to improve that industry's safety regulations.

One incident that focused on the need to change the state abortion statutes occurred in 1962. Sherri Finkbine, a local television actress in Arizona, married and the mother of four young children, was pregnant with her fifth child when she learned that the Thalidomide tranquilizer she had taken caused severe birth defects such as inhibiting the growth of any fetal limbs. Though never approved by the Federal Drug Administration, Thalidomide was obtained in Europe and used by women in the United States, many of whom had used it during pregnancy.

As soon as Ms. Finkbine suspected she had taken a dangerous drug, she made an appointment to see her obstetrician, informing him of the Thalidomide usage. He confirmed that Thalidomide had been the culprit in numerous deformed babies and that Ms. Finkbine had taken the strongest possible dosage. He advised her to have an abortion and set up the appointment for the following Monday.

When she returned home, Ms. Finkbine thought about other servicemen who had been to Germany and who, like her husband, might also have brought their wives Thalidomide to take. Her conscience and her experience with the media prompted her to tell her story to a journalist, hoping it would save other women from a similar plight.

The story hit the papers over the weekend. Wire

stories carried it all over the country. Although Ms. Finkbine had not revealed her name in the article, on Monday, when she was ready for her abortion, she learned that the hospital where it had been scheduled to take place had suddenly rescinded her appointment, denying her permission to have an abortion and failing to give her any reason. The reason, Ms. Finkbine suspected, was the publicity that had ensued over her case.

Thousands of people wrote to Ms. Finkbine, most of whom supported her decision to have an abortion, although a few condemned her. Ms. Finkbine, however, was unable to obtain an abortion in her homestate or anywhere else in the United States. She applied for a visa to Japan, where abortion on demand was legal. Japan denied her the visa, perhaps to avoid involvement in an international moral controversy. Four months pregnant and convinced of the need to terminate her pregnancy, Ms. Finkbine and her husband flew to Sweden, where therapeutic abortions were legal if a medical board reviewed the case and granted permission. Eventually, Ms. Finkbine was given permission, and she had the abortion. The autopsy performed on the fetus revealed such extensive deformity that her Swedish doctor informed her that the fetus would never have survived. After her ordeal was over, Ms. Finkbine conceived again, and she soon gave birth to a healthy baby.

Another incident soon drew attention to the abortion issue. This time a national epidemic of German measles (rubella) broke out. Although German measles is generally considered to be an innocuous disease, if it is contracted during the first sixteen weeks of pregnancy, it causes severe disabilities, including heart defects, blindness, and deafness in 30–50 percent of the babies born. Between 1962 and 1965, over 80,000 pregnant women contracted German measles. Many of them sought legal abortions but were denied them. Others had illegal abortions, but 15,000 women gave birth to babies with severe disabilities.[3]

There were doctors who were willing to perform abortions on women exposed to German measles, even though it meant that they were jeopardizing their careers if caught. In 1965, a Roman Catholic doctor who was head of the California State Medical Board threatened any doctors with loss of license if caught performing abortions on these women. He instigated an investigation that found nine doctors from San Francisco guilty of performing illegal abortions, and he promised to implicate an additional thirty-nine physicians. From all across the nation, over two thousand doctors, including many medical school deans, rallied to the support of the indicted physicians. Thousands of other people joined their cause as well. A movement ensued to liberalize California's abortion statute, after which a bill was introduced into the state legislature.

Just before the bill passed in California, another state, Colorado, passed a statute that liberalized its abortion laws, a statute consistent with the guidelines of the Model Penal Code. Several other states followed and reformed their laws, and four—New York, Hawaii, Alaska, and Washington—actually went beyond the Model Penal Code's recommendation and virtually legalized abortion on demand during the first three months of pregnancy.

Once legal abortion was available and the tight restrictions had been lifted, at least in some of the states, the number of legal abortions skyrocketed. It went from less than ten thousand in the early '60s to three-quarters of a million by 1972. California alone accounted for 100,000 abortions each year.

During the years of legislative reform, the issue began to grow from a limited concern of doctors to protect themselves from criminal penalties and to offer women safe abortions to a broader issue of social equality.

Changing societal mores and the liberalization of some of the states' abortion laws during the 1960s and early 1970s enabled women to feel more comfortable discussing their abortions. For what had once been taken for granted to be a personal ordeal was increasingly being perceived as a larger outrage, an injustice against women as a group.

When abortion was illegal, women terminated their unwanted pregnancies secretly, dangerously, shamefully. But as soon as women began asserting themselves, demanding more than the traditional roles of housewife and "pink collar" worker (the low-paying jobs like secretary, store clerk, and clerical worker), demanding that motherhood be a choice, not a requirement, even demanding freedom in sexuality, women began to expect to control their own bodies and their own fertility. Abortion was no longer just a personal matter to take care of an unwanted pregnancy; it emerged as a rallying point for social change and equality.

Famous women held press conferences and gave interviews in which they poignantly revealed their own illegal abortion experiences. Other women collected thousands upon thousands of petitions and signatures. Still others marched, demonstrated, and performed in street theaters, where they handed out red-painted coat hangers symbolic of the dangerous self-induced illegal abortions to which they had subjected themselves in the absence of legal abortion.

Not everyone wanted to merely reform the state laws; some people wanted to totally repeal them. "Abortion on demand," they insisted. Nothing less was acceptable. For them, compulsory pregnancy was analogous to slavery.

Women demanded the same education, the same jobs, the same opportunities in life as men. No longer content to assume separate roles in life or the traditional ones expected of them simply because they were born female, they demanded equality. One measure of that equality, they asserted, was the right to have an abortion upon demand.

Groups like the American Civil Liberties Union (ACLU), which sympathized with the quest for equality, and the Planned Parenthood League, which supported a woman's right to legal abortion, contributed huge sums of money and legal expertise to the cause.

Restless from waiting for legislative change in the abortion laws, and taking a cue from the Civil Rights movement that had succeeded in gaining enormous strides through landmark Supreme Court decisions such as *Brown* v. *the Board of Education,* abortion reformers decided to wage a litigation campaign to overturn the state statutes. This was a carefully executed legal campaign that flooded the lower courts with abortion cases, some of which the abortion supporters hoped would ultimately reach the Supreme Court.

Actually, two cases dealing with the right to use contraception paved the way for abortion reform. The first was a repeal of the 1876 Comstock Law, which, as discussed previously, had dealt not just with obscenity but with the distribution and sale of birth control, making it illegal even for married couples to procure it through the mail. Then, in *Griswold* v. *Connecticut,* the Supreme Court ruled that a married couple was entitled to the right to privacy and should be guaranteed full protection from government intrusion on matters as private as contraception and whether to have a child. In 1972, in a subsequent ruling *(Eisenstadt* v. *Baird),* the Supreme Court extended this right to privacy to single persons. This right to privacy was an important decision because it became the foundation for what would be the Court's later decision on abortion.

The Supreme Court is rather selective about the cases it will hear. Probably because so many abortion cases were flooding the lower courts and because of the mounting public controversy over abortion that was substantially eroding support for the existing state laws, the Supreme Court decided to hear two abortion cases. Its decision to rule on the cases has been sharply criticized by scholars who believe that abortion is beyond the Supreme Court's jurisdiction and ought to remain in the realm of state law.

Late in 1971, the court agreed to hear two cases, *Roe* v. *Wade* and *Doe* v. *Bolton*. *Roe* v. *Wade* specifically challenged the Texas statute denying all but life-saving abortions. *Doe* v. *Bolton* challenged the Georgia statute for imposing such restrictive medical requirements and allowing hospitals to impose abortion quotas, limiting the number of abortions that could be performed in a given month. The Court charged that, in effect, they denied a woman the right to the legal abortion to which she was entitled. Although these cases challenged specific state laws, they also raised much broader issues, like the issue of whether a woman's right to an abortion was legal and protected by the Constitution.

Jane Roe and Mary Doe (both pseudonyms) were the plaintiffs, the parties challenging the state. Because they actually represented millions of women like themselves for whom the state statutes denied legal abortion, their cases were called class action suits.

In both of the cases, a declaratory judgment was sought. This is a ruling that permits a court to review a law by listening to testimony and reading legal briefs on why the law should be struck down. The existing law did not have to be broken to be challenged. (Breaking it, in fact, a person would risk criminal prosecution and sentencing if found guilty.) By seeking declaratory judgment, Jane Roe, Mary Doe, and the other parties in their case could test the law without breaking it.

Because abortion is so complex and controversial an issue, it took the Supreme Court over a year to rule on the case. The majority opinion, the written rule on a case, which becomes law and the basis for settling future disputes, was written by Justice Harry A. Blackmun, chosen because of his experience in medical law.

Justice Blackmun wished to write a judgment that would be general enough to include all the controversies in the issue but specific enough to be a solid legal document on which to settle future legal debates.

After a second hearing in October 1972, Justice Blackmun finished writing the opinion, and a final vote was taken. On January 22, 1973, in a 7–2 vote, the Supreme Court struck down both the Texas and Georgia statutes. Abortion was legalized in a ruling so sweeping and so liberal that it surprised even those who had wanted it. It outraged those who had not.

Chapter Two

ROE V. WADE

The *Roe* v. *Wade* ruling struck down all those state abortion laws that had been more restrictive than this new law, creating a national standard of abortion laws for the entire nation.

Like many rulings, there are still issues not addressed: issues such as whether a minor can have an abortion without her parents' consent or notification; whether the federal government has to subsidize abortions for low-income women; and how much the state can regulate the safety of the procedure. Many of these issues have been resolved in subsequent cases before the Supreme Court. Some issues are currently in litigation and the remainder will be part of future debate.

ROE V. *WADE*

- The right to privacy includes a woman's decision to have an abortion.
- The right to have an abortion is not absolute; state laws may regulate the medical standards in order to safeguard the woman's health during the procedure.

As the fetus develops, the state may have an interest in protecting its life.

- The unborn are not included in the definition of "person" in the Fourteenth Amendment and, therefore, have no constitutional rights.

- During the first trimester (the first three months of pregnancy), a woman is entitled to an abortion. The state may insist that she consult with a physician, but the final decision on whether to have an abortion must be hers alone.

- Until the point in the pregnancy where the fetus is *viable* (capable of life outside the womb, usually between twenty-four and twenty-eight weeks, although some states set it closer to twenty-two weeks), the state may only regulate abortions to preserve or protect maternal health. (The state cannot require that abortions be done in a hospital, only that they be performed in a medical setting by a licensed physician.)

- When the fetus is viable, the state may prohibit abortions except when it is necessary to preserve the mother's life or health.

- The state may insist that abortions only be performed by licensed physicians.

Right to Privacy. The Court's decision was based on a woman's right to privacy, which the Court ruled is a basic civil right. Privacy in matters of whether to have a child was first recognized in the two previous contraception cases, *Griswold* v. *Connecticut* and *Eisenstadt* v. *Baird*.

The right to privacy is not specifically written into the body of the Constitution or the Bill of Rights. In fact, when Justice White, who dissented in *Roe* v. *Wade*, wrote his dissenting opinion, he claimed that he could find "nothing in the language or history of the Constitution to support the Court's judgment." He continued his argument saying, "The Court simply fashions and announces a new constitutional right for pregnant women."

Many constitutional scholars agree with Justice White. These scholars believe that the Supreme Court should not attempt to "rewrite" the Constitution but should merely interpret what is already there. Those who oppose the ruling in *Roe* v. *Wade* claim that the Court was indeed writing new amendments and granting new rights.

But there is a way to justify "new rights" without writing new amendments. Some rights, though not written, can be "interpreted" or "alluded" from what is already written, and it is up to the Court to determine just what is alluded. These rights are called *penumbras* of the Bill of Rights. (Penumbra literally means "the dark side of the moon, the part we cannot see.") The penumbras of the Bill of Rights are those which the Court has determined are understood but not expressly written.

The Supreme Court decided that several of the amendments, namely, the first, fifth, ninth, and fourteenth, support a woman's right to an abortion. The Justices based this decision on the right to "personal privacy" established in two previous cases, *Griswold* v. *Connecticut* and *Eisenstadt* v. *Baird*.

The right to privacy, whether it be founded in the Fourteenth Amendment's concept of personal liberty and restrictions upon state action or in the Ninth Amendment's reservation of the rights to the people, is broad enough to encompass a woman's decision whether or not to terminate her pregnancy.[1]

Although the parties challenging the states' laws insisted that a woman should be entitled to an abortion at "whatever time, in whatever way, and for whatever reason she alone chooses" (abortion on demand), the Supreme Court disagreed with such an unrestrictive right. It claimed that the state could regulate where and by whom the abortion was done, but only enough to ensure that the woman was having a medically safe abortion.

The Court also insisted that a person does not have an unlimited right to do as she pleases with her own body. There comes a point in pregnancy, the point of viability, when a fetus can survive life outside the womb. At this point, a woman does *not* have complete control of her body and is entitled to an abortion only if the abortion is to save her life or preserve her health. What the Supreme Court did not specify was what exactly constitutes a threat to health that would warrant aborting a viable fetus. In fact, the wording is so ambiguous and subject to interpretation that opponents of abortion argue that abortion is virtually legal during an entire pregnancy.

Personhood. Because people who were trained in medicine, philosophy, and theology could not reach agreement on when life begins, the Court decided that neither should it. In addition, it claimed that the Constitution never defined what the word "person" included. The Court did rule, however, that the word "person" as used in the Fourteenth Amendment did not include the unborn. Perhaps more than any other statement the Court made, this outraged abortion opponents.

Trimesters. The Court recognizes that as pregnancy progresses, the fetus develops until it is capable of survival outside the mother's womb. At that point, the Court said the fetus legally deserves to have its life protected.

During the first and second trimester, an abortion is legal, for any reason, if it is performed by a licensed

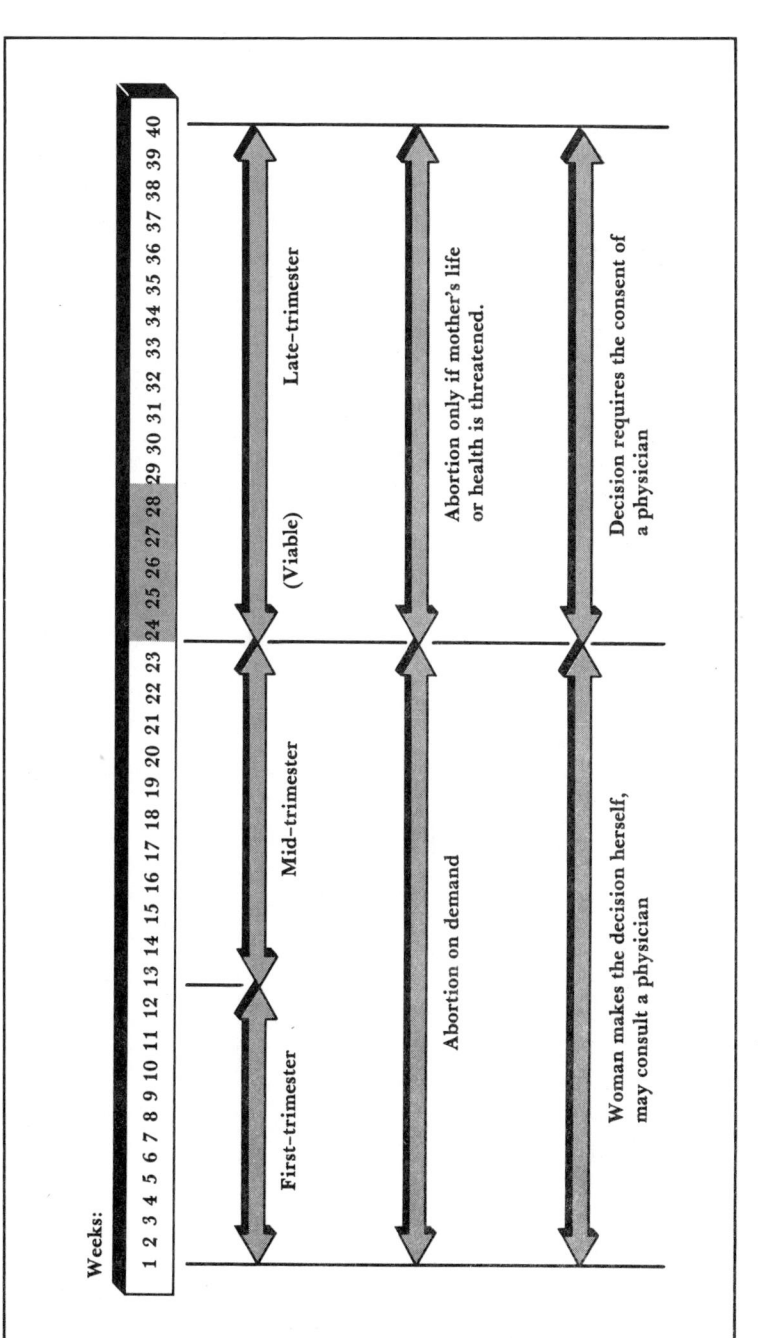

physician in a medical setting, which includes hospitals, physicians' private offices, and clinics not associated with a hospital.

After the point at which a fetus is viable, a state may, in the interest of the fetus's life, prohibit a woman from having an abortion unless her life or health is threatened by the pregnancy. This decision is ultimately that of the woman's physician. This point was set at the end of the second trimester, between twenty-four and twenty-eight weeks, but it was based on what was medically possible in 1973. Today, with improvements in the type of care available to premature infants, viability has moved closer to twenty-two weeks.

State Regulation. The state is entitled to establish regulations to ensure that abortions are medically safe, but it may not establish such strict guidelines that a woman cannot obtain an abortion. The states are also permitted to enact laws that regulate abortions if those laws do not limit any rights to which the woman is entitled under *Roe* v. *Wade*. If a state passes a law that is too restrictive, and many states have, then that law can be challenged in court. The courts hear the case and determine whether to strike down or uphold the state's law.

Though no states had to pass any new laws—the Supreme Court decision is the "law of the land"—many, in fact, did pass them. In 1973, the year of the decision, over two hundred bills were introduced into state legislatures, and almost half of them were so restrictive, they were struck down in court.[2]

Although these new laws could not criminalize abortion, they did attempt to restrict it, especially where minors are concerned.

Consent. Many states enacted laws that compelled a woman seeking an abortion to have the consent of her spouse, the father, or if she were a minor, her parents.

States may require that a woman consult a doctor, but they cannot require that a woman have anyone else's consent or permission to have an abortion—not the father, her doctor, or the state. A state can make an exception in the case of minors, and at least twenty states have. Though a parent cannot force his or her daughter to have an abortion, many states require that those minors who are *unemancipated* (still living with their parents or guardians and dependent on them) obtain their parent's (or guardian's) consent in order to have an abortion.

Though some teenagers feel they can at least ask one of their parents for permission, many feel unable to do so. One young girl in Minnesota told the court that she could not go to her parents, "because my mother has a documented past of severe mental illness . . . my father has a violent temper . . . and probably would have hit me."

If a young woman feels she cannot ask for her parent's permission, then the Supreme Court has decided that because her right to have an abortion does not depend on her age, she should have an alternative way to make the decision. She can judicially bypass the consent requirement, which means that she can go to court and have the court decide whether or not she is mature enough to make an informed decision. (Only if the court decides she is too immature to make her own decision, which almost never happens, will a judge then rule on whether an abortion is in her best interest.)

In one celebrated case in 1981 in Minnesota, a mother denied permission for her eleven-year-old to have an abortion. The girl went to court, where the judge ruled she was not mature enough to make the decision, and it was in her best interest not to have an abortion. This ruling upset many people who believe that if a child is too young to make her own decision about whether or not she should have a baby, she is also too young to deal with pregnancy or motherhood.

Going to court is a hardship for many young women, often causing them much more emotional stress than the abortion itself. Since many have to delay their abortions until after their court appearance, the procedure itself is then riskier and often more costly. In some cases, this proves such a hardship that the women simply don't have abortions.

A recent case, *Hodgson v. Minnesota,* challenged this parental consent law, charging that the hardships incurred from the law outweigh the benefits to the family they were intended to preserve. The statute was struck down in the lower courts and, as this book goes to press, is scheduled to be heard by the United States Supreme Court.

Informed Consent. When a person undergoes any medical procedure, informed consent is a standard requirement; it informs the patient of all of the risks of the procedure. When a woman is contemplating an abortion, she must be informed of the procedure and of its risks.

Although several states have enacted statutes that require all information about the development of the fetus or what the fetus undergoes during the procedure be told to the woman, these statutes have been struck down by the Supreme Court. The Court has determined that while the woman must be informed of the medical risks to herself, she does not have to hear about the fetus. The Court ruled that such information is "speculative," and that a woman can safely undergo an abortion without knowing exactly how her fetus looks and what it is capable of doing.

But abortion is unlike any other medical procedure in that it does affect more than the woman; it affects her fetus. Having an abortion is not the same as having a tonsillectomy. Although some people believe that information about the fetus will not alter a woman's decision but will only upset her more than she may already be, others point to that group of women who do change their minds about having an abortion when they are confronted with all the facts. This remains still another controversy in the abortion issue, and as the following testimony documents, the lack of informed consent causes some women a great deal of anguish, guilt, or remorse.

> Had I been counselled properly concerning the pain and the development of my unborn child, I doubt that I would have chosen abortion. I was not forewarned of the health risks or the deep psychological aftereffects of abortion. As a bright college graduate, I had a promising future ahead of me. Following my abortion, I became deeply depressed, suicidal, and unable to hold a job. I never mourned the loss of my appendix, so why did I grieve over the passing of an enigmatic uterine blob? The answer is that it wasn't a mere "blob of tissue." It was a living baby. I realized it the moment I saw his dismembered body. I realized it too late."[3]

Notification. Notification means that when a woman has an abortion, either the spouse or family must be notified within twenty-four hours of the procedure. Other statutes have stated that a minor's parent or guardian must be notified of her decision to have an abortion, and then she must wait twenty-four hours before having one.

But all notification requirements, with the exception of the one pertaining to these "unemancipated" minors, have been struck down as unconstitutional. The *Hartigan v. Zbaraz* case currently before the Supreme Court deals specifically with this issue of parental notification.

Conscience Clause. In another decision, the Supreme Court ruled that no physician or hospital, even publicly funded institutions, can be compelled to perform abortions if it goes against their moral beliefs. Many physicians and hospitals have exercised this option by refusing to do any abortions or to do abortions late in pregnancy.

Advertising. A few states tried to limit abortion clinics from advertising their services, which many do, both on public billboards and in the *Yellow Pages,* for example, but the Supreme Court struck down this restriction, claiming that it infringes on a business's right to free speech.

OVERTURNING
ROE V. WADE

Make no mistake, abortion-on-demand is not a right granted by the Constitution. No serious scholar, including one disposed to agree with the Court's result, has argued that the framers of the Constitution intended to create such a right.

—Ronald Reagan

Throughout its history, the Supreme Court has overturned over one hundred decisions. Like Ronald Reagan, the Justices who opposed the *Roe* v. *Wade* decision believed that the Court had stretched beyond its constitutional limits by including the right to abortion as part of the right to privacy, which itself was never written into the Constitution. The two Justices who dissented in *Roe* v. *Wade,* Rehnquist and White, were prepared to overrule it immediately, even though the Court cannot overrule a decision until it has an appropriate case before it. The Court has not had such a case.

This ad for an abortion clinic appeared in a 1978 edition of a student newspaper at Boston College, a Roman Catholic school in Newton, Massachusetts. College officials at the time ordered the newspaper to move off campus for printing the advertisement.

Though some legal scholars uphold the woman's right to privacy, they fail to see how abortion is encompassed in that right. Others believe that regardless of whether a woman should be entitled to an abortion, it is for the states, not the Supreme Court, to decide.

Abortion is a medical procedure with one goal: to terminate a pregnancy. Basing predictions on recent technological advances that have enabled premature infants to survive outside the womb earlier and earlier in their gestation, futurists have predicted that someday it might be possible to remove a fetus from its mother prior to viability and somehow provide an artificial womb. Others have suggested that a fetus could be transplanted into an infertile woman.

What is most significant in view of the tremendous advances that have been made is that it will be necessary to come to terms with exactly what is meant by abortion. The Supreme Court has failed to address this distinction between terminating pregnancy and terminating the life of a fetus.

Another problem with the Court's ruling is the issue of viability. Though only a small percentage of twenty-six-week-old fetuses survived outside the womb when the decision was written in 1973, more than half survive now. Viability is being pushed earlier than ever. The most significant problem premature infants have in surviving is the immaturity of their lungs; they lack the substance that prevents their lungs from collapsing after each breath. This lack of "surfactant" is a major cause of premature infant mortality. Researchers are working towards the discovery of a synthetic surfactant. Although some are pessimistic that it can be developed, there are others who speculate that not only can it be discovered but that such a discovery would move viability even earlier.

What all this means for *Roe* v. *Wade* is that through medical technology, the basis for the decision could be invalid and the decision would have to be reversed, or else a new decision based on new legal criteria would have to be written. For these technological reasons, Justice Sandra O'Connor wrote in a dissent of one of the abortion cases that "*Roe* v. *Wade* was on a collision course with itself."

HUMAN LIFE AMENDMENT

Efforts have been made to abolish legal abortion with the introduction of an amendment that would give the fetus the status of a "person" from the moment of conception and entitle it to protection (and the right to life) under the Constitution. Although such a *Human Life amendment* would be difficult to enforce, it would certainly make abortion illegal. Such legislation has been introduced and defeated several times.

Another proposed amendment to the Constitution is the *States' Rights Amendment*. Its authors would like to restore the power to pass laws governing abortion back to the state legislatures, trusting that many states, if not all, would subsequently restrict or criminalize abortion. If the laws varied from state to state, however, the result would be a mosaic of abortion statutes. Some states might become "abortion mills," as California and New York were in danger of becoming prior to 1973, while other states would outlaw abortion.

Are any of these amendments likely to be passed? Amendments require a two-thirds majority vote from both the House of Representatives and the Senate to pass, or else a two-thirds vote from all the state legislatures (thirty-four states) in order to call for a Constitutional Convention, at which time a new amendment could be drafted. If a new amendment were to be drafted at a Constitutional Convention, it would require three-fourths of the state legislatures to approve it in order to be ratified.

Certainly it is possible, if not always conceivable, that abortion could someday be illegal or more restrictive. Dozens of decisions since *Roe* v. *Wade* as well as a number of national referendums have attempted just that. Public support for the ruling could erode, and medical technology could outdate the basis for the decision. On more than a hundred occasions, the Supreme Court has reversed its decisions. In the meantime, abortion continues to play time in the legal arena, and a starring role in the legislative future is always a possibility.

Chapter Three

HOW ABORTIONS ARE PERFORMED

> The abortion itself was amazingly quick and painless (considering the propaganda to the contrary). I spent an hour lying down to recover. I remember being so elated—it was over and it had been so simple.

> It hurt so much. It was incredible. The people at the clinic were really sweet and helpful but they should have told me how much it was going to hurt. What hurt the most was that I could feel when they were scraping around inside. I've talked to a lot of girls who said the same thing happened to them when they were really far along. That's why it pays to have an abortion as early as possible.[1]

After a woman's egg has been fertilized by a sperm, the *zygote,* as the fertilized egg is now called, travels down her Fallopian tube, enters her uterus, and implants itself in her uterine wall. For the next two months, it is medically referred to as an *embryo,* and after that as a *fetus,* as it continues growing into what will eventually become a baby.

But not all fertilized eggs, zygotes, embryos, or fetuses make it to the baby stage. In fact, about half of all the fertilized eggs fail to become implanted in the very beginning and are discharged from the body or absorbed back into it. Things can still happen to the eggs that do implant and continue growing. Sometimes, the embryo or fetus fails to develop properly, and it is naturally expelled, or forced out. When this occurs less than twenty-six weeks after conception, the expulsion is called a *spontaneous abortion*. After twenty-six weeks, it is called a *miscarriage* or *premature birth*. It is common for a pregnancy to end in spontaneous abortion or miscarriage; it happens to one out of every six pregnant women. For the woman or couple who want to have a baby, a spontaneous abortion or miscarriage can be traumatic and can even cause as much grief as if a child already born had died.

One form of birth control is to force the fertilized egg to be expelled from the body before implantation. Taking the pill, D.E.S. (the "morning-after-pill," frequently administered to victims of rape), or wearing an I.U.D. (intrauterine device) will prevent the zygote from implantation. In addition, a new drug, RU 486, also interferes with implantation, though in a different way. While these artificial methods of forcing the zygote to be expelled or reabsorbed are usually classified as birth control because they are effective *after* fertilization, they are also referred to as *abortifacients*.

Once the fetus has been firmly attached to the uterus and has developed a placenta, the protective sac in which it will receive all its nourishment, including oxygen, deliberately forcing it to be expelled out of the womb is called *induced abortion*. If an abortion is induced for medical reasons (to protect a woman's health or even save her life), it is called a *therapeutic induced abortion*. If it is performed for a nonmedical reason, it is called a *non-therapeutic induced abortion,* or an *elective abortion.*

THE FEMALE REPRODUCTIVE SYSTEM

SIDE VIEW

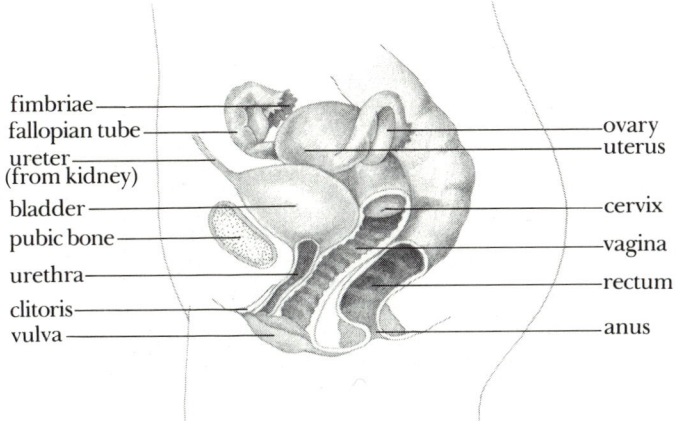

FRONT VIEW

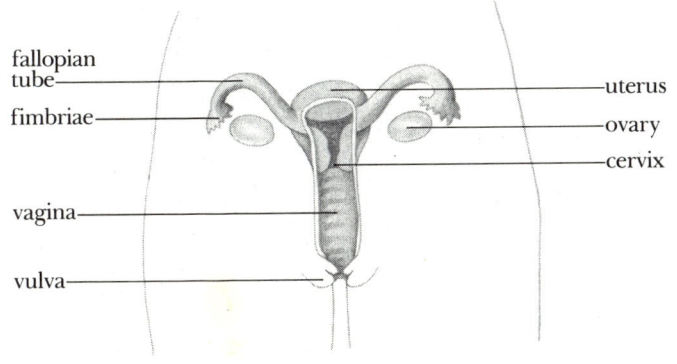

Abortions can be induced by using a variety of chemical, herbal, mechanical, or surgical methods. Many of these methods, though they produce an abortion, are also risky and can even be fatal. For example, women used to drink toxic potions that brought on such severe nausea and diarrhea, they would have an abortion. In some primitive societies, women engage in stressful physical activity, including having others trample on their bellies, to induce abortion. Such methods are dangerous and don't always induce an abortion. In the United States, all legal induced abortions must be medical procedures performed by licensed physicians in medical settings.

Today, the majority of abortions are performed in the first twelve weeks of pregnancy, half in fact, by the eighth week. *Instrumental evacuation,* when the cervix (opening of the uterus) is *dilated* (stretched) and the fetus and placenta are removed, is used in 98 percent of all abortions. It is the safest method available, safer than a tonsillectomy.

As pregnancy progresses into the second trimester, the abortion is accomplished by either inducing premature labor and causing the woman to deliver the fetus and placenta, or else surgically removing the fetus and placenta. About 80 percent of late abortions are performed by the first method; the remainder, which account for only a fraction of all abortions, are rarely performed because such surgery carries the greatest risk of any abortion procedure and is rarely required.

Before an abortion is performed, a pregnancy test is done to confirm the pregnancy. If the test is positive and the woman is pregnant, then the *gestation,* or how far along she is in the pregnancy, is determined. Because the exact moment an egg is fertilized is impossible to pinpoint accurately, the gestation is measured from the date of a woman's last period. Referred to as

	Average Fetal Development (Fertilization Age)	Information	Percentage of Abortions Performed
FIRST TRIMESTER	3 Weeks	Earliest point at which pregnancy can be determined.	
	4 Weeks: Fetus is 1/5 of an inch in length.		
	8 Weeks: Fetus is approximately 1 inch long.		51.5% of all abortions performed in first 8 weeks after fertilization.
	10 Weeks: Fetus is approximately 2 inches long and weighs 1/2 ounce.	Chorionic Villus Biopsy, a new pre-natal diagnostic procedure, is now being tested in medical centers around the country. This procedure involves taking a sample of fetal tissue as early as 10 weeks gestation. It requires no anesthetic and is painless. However, it is associated with a 3-9% miscarriage rate, making continued research necessary before it can be made widely available.*	91.3% of all abortions are performed in first 10 weeks after fertilization.
SECOND TRIMESTER	12 Weeks: Fetus is approximately 3 1/2 inches in length and weighs 1.5 ounces.		
	13-16 Weeks: Fetus is 5 1/2 inches in length and weighs 7 oz. at 16 weeks.	Amniocentesis performed between 15 and 18 weeks. This procedure involves the withdrawal of a small amount of the amniotic fluid which surrounds the fetus; chromosomes in cells in this fluid are then analyzed for specific birth defects.	97% of all abortions are performed by the end of 14 weeks after fertilization. 2.7% of all abortions are performed shortly after 15 weeks after fertilization.
	18 Weeks: Fetus is 6 inches in length and weighs 11 ounces.	Amniocentesis results become available after 2-6 week period.	
	20 Weeks: Fetus is 7 1/2 inches and weighs approximately 16 oz.		
THIRD TRIMESTER	24 Weeks: Fetus is 9 inches in length and weighs 1 3/4 pounds.	Earliest possible point of viability.** Defined as the point at which the fetus can survive outside the womb without life support systems.	Few major hospitals will perform abortions at this stage of fetal development unless the life of the woman is at stake.
	38-40 Weeks: Full-term delivery; fetus is approximately 19 inches long and weighs 6-9 pounds.		

*For additional information, see *Family Planning Perspectives*, 'Vol. 15, No. 6, November/December 1983, p. 284.

**There is no sharp limit of development, age, or weight at which a fetus automatically becomes viable or beyond which survival is assured, but experience has shown that it is rare for a baby to survive whose weight is less than 17 oz. or whose fertilization age is less than 22 weeks. (Moore)

Fetal development figures from *The Developing Human* (3rd Edition), by Dr. Keith L. Moore, 1982; W. B. Sanders Co.

an LMP ("last menstrual period"), it is actually two weeks older than the fetus, because a fetus is not usually fertilized until two weeks *after* the last menstrual period. Thus, a ten-week LMP is only an eight-week fetus.

If a woman's periods are irregular, if she has "spotted" during the first few months of her pregnancy (a common occurrence), or if a woman appears further along than her LMP suggests, then doctors might perform additional tests to verify the gestation. They will either measure her uterus during a physical examination or analyze the fetus's development by an *ultrasound* test, just to make sure that they don't perform an abortion on a viable fetus or use a procedure that is inappropriate.

EARLY ABORTION PROCEDURES

An abortion can be performed as early as the first week or two. But due to the microscopic size of the embryo at this stage, performing a *menstrual extraction,* as such procedures are called, is rarely done. The embryo is so small it is easy to miss, and the procedure results in an incomplete abortion. Moreover, pregnancy cannot be accurately confirmed so early, and thus a woman might have a procedure that she doesn't actually need.

Another early abortion method is a recently developed one, RU 486. Developed by a French biochemist, Dr. Etienne-Emile Beaulieu, RU 486 works by blocking the fertilized egg from implanting itself in the uterine

As one of the first steps in the abortion procedure, this young woman is having her blood pressure taken at an abortion clinic.

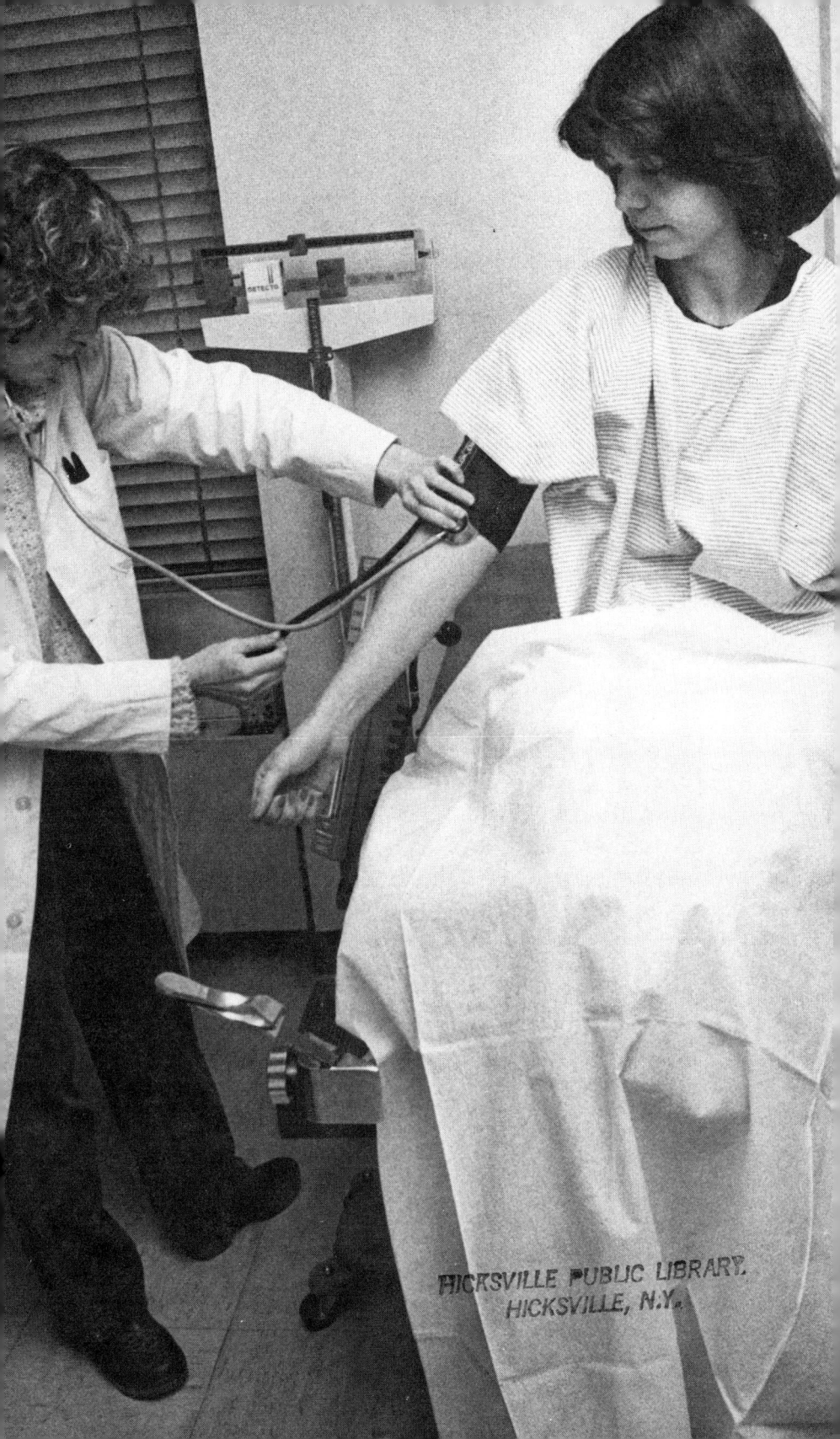

wall, causing the lining to break away as in a normal menstrual cycle and expel the egg-zygote. Like menstrual extraction, RU 486 results in a percentage of incomplete abortions (5–10 percent during the first few weeks; up to 30 percent by the fifth week). Although it can be combined with the hormone prostaglandin to improve its rate of success, prostaglandin causes unpleasant side effects. Some people regard RU 486 as birth control, but given its cost and the occasional side effect of excessive bleeding that causes some women to be hospitalized, its future as a birth control method is dubious. Still, despite its drawbacks and current unavailability in the United States, RU 486 holds new options for women seeking abortions. As its inventor, Dr. Beaulieu, forecasts, "Abortion should more or less disappear as a concept."[2]

Currently, the safest, most reliable abortions are performed between seven and ten weeks LMP. When abortion services are legal and available, the tendency everywhere is for women to obtain them as early as possible during this safe period. For as pregnancy continues beyond this period, the uterus grows increasingly larger and softer, making abortions more complicated and riskier.

INSTRUMENTAL EVACUATION

Perhaps the safest procedure, accounting for more than 90 percent of all abortions, is the vacuum aspiration, a procedure that was developed in recent decades. During a vacuum aspiration, the cervix, or opening to the uterus, is first numbed, and then gently stretched, or *dilated,* using *dilators* (rods) or sterile *lamanaria,* a special seaweed formed into rods. Dilation with dilators takes only a few minutes; dilation with lamanaria takes up to twenty-four hours, but is much gentler and less traumatic.

After the cervix has been dilated, a *cannula* or small tube with an opening or two is inserted into the uterus. The *aspirator,* which is the vacuum machine that creates suction to empty the uterus and complete the abortion, is connected to the cannula by tubing. If dilators are used, as they usually are, then an entire vacuum aspiration abortion takes less than half an hour, usually only fifteen minutes.

Some women experience only mild cramping during a vacuum abortion, while others report intense pain and cramping. In Linda Bird Francke's book, *The Ambivalence of Abortion,* one woman said that during her abortion she "practiced breathing and really mellowed out and experienced no pain,"[3] while another woman said that her abortion was "incredibly painful."[4]

Another type of evacuation method that was widely used prior to the development of the vacuum aspiration is *dilation and curettage.* Although it is seldom used anymore for first trimester abortions, it is still the preferred method for those abortions performed during the twelfth or thirteenth week of pregnancy.

LATE ABORTION PROCEDURES

Fewer than one out of ten women has an abortion after the first trimester; less than one out of a hundred after twenty weeks LMP. Given the difficulty of determining exact fetal age, many physicians are reluctant to perform abortions after the twentieth week because of the fear that they might end up performing an abortion on a viable fetus. Also, as sociologist Jonathan Imber found in his study of physicians, many doctors are reluctant to perform abortions on second trimester fetuses that are developed enough to bear what they consider a striking resemblance to the babies they also deliver.

Between the thirteenth and fifteenth week of pregnancy, *dilation and evacuation* (D & E), a method similar to vacuum aspiration, is the preferred method. After the first trimester, the fetus is too large to pass through the cannula during a vacuum aspiration and must be dismembered by using instruments. This process can be so stressful that many professionals express ambivalence towards performing such abortions, while others, despite supporting a woman's choice to have an abortion, refuse to participate in the procedure.

An advantage of the D & E over other later procedures is that it can be done on an outpatient basis. In addition, it only takes half an hour or less to perform.

Though it cannot be performed until the sixteenth week because the ambiotic sac that surrounds the fetus is too small to accurately locate, *medical induction* or *instillation* is the preferred method for later abortions. During instillation, a chemical such as saline solution or prostaglandin is "instilled" or injected into a woman's womb, causing her to go into premature labor and expel the fetus and placenta. Labor can last for hours, even days, and is often a painful and emotionally draining ordeal. By the fourth or fifth month, many women having abortions have already felt their fetus move or seen it on sonogram screens.

> I was given a saline abortion at four months, and I never once was told of the pain involved during the injection of the saline solution into my womb. Neither was I told of the pain involved in labor, nor even that my body would go into labor to reject the struggling, dying baby that was being burned alive in my uterus. Over four hours after the injection, I gave birth to my dead son. I know he was my son because I asked the nurse what it was as she removed the bedpan, and she said, "It's a boy."[5]

One of the most distressing drawbacks of performing an instillation using the hormone prostaglandin is the possibility of having the fetus born alive. Unless a substance like saline solution or urea (another toxic substance) is given in conjunction with the prostaglandin or else an injection is used that stops the fetal heartbeat, there is no guarantee against a viable fetus being born, though it occurs only rarely. For those opposing abortion, there is no moral distinction between a fetus that dies during an abortion and infanticide. Even for those in support of a woman's choice to have an abortion, the odds of delivering a live fetus, however small, are enough to dissuade them from performing abortions, as mentioned previously.

When a fetus is born alive, all measures are taken to save its life. The Supreme Court has ruled that a state may legally require another physician, typically a pediatrician, to be present during late abortions in case of a live birth.

In rare cases, abortions are performed on women diagnosed with cancer of the uterus or other serious medical problems. In these cases, the abortion is surgically performed in either a hysterotomy or a hysterectomy. In a hysterotomy, both the fetus and placenta are surgically removed, while in a hysterectomy, reproductive organs like the uterus and ovaries may be removed as well. Because such abortions are risky and only used in emergencies, they are rare and account for less than 1 percent of all abortions.

COMPLICATIONS

Abortions are one of the most medically safe surgical procedures, but like all surgical procedures, not without risk. With the exception of teenagers for whom abortion is actually seven to nine times as safe as childbirth, overall, it carries the same medical risk as childbirth.

Primarily, it has been the legalization of abortion that has contributed to the reduction of risk. Other factors include the shift to abortions earlier in the pregnancy, to the use of vacuum aspiration, local anesthesia, and most important, to the growing expertise of physicians in performing abortions.

The most frequent complications of abortion include infection, blood clots, excessive bleeding, tears in the cervix, perforation of the uterine wall, and, in later abortions, amniotic fluid embolism. This happens when the amniotic fluid enters the bloodstream and goes to the heart, where it can cause death.

In first-trimester abortions, only about two or three out of a hundred women complain of minor complications, and less than one out of a hundred has a complication severe enough to warrant additional surgery or hospitalization.[6] Later abortions carry greater risk, but even those are not as substantial as the risks that women experienced prior to the legalization of abortion.

POST ABORTION SYNDROME

In her classical study of the way women make moral decisions about abortion, Carol Gilligan found that abortion is hardly undertaken without serious consideration. But the decision does come at a time when a woman may be nauseous, extremely tired, and emotionally sensitive. Some women are abandoned by their companions after announcing their pregnancy, while others may be compelled to deal with disappointed or angry parents. This period can be and often is a traumatic time in a woman's life.

Though many women are relieved to have abortions, others are not. These women can suffer from what has been diagnosed as Post Abortion Syndrome, or PAS, a depression that is a direct result of having an abortion. There is much controversy over the impact of abortion on a woman's emotional health, and so PAS is not universally recognized by the psychiatric community. Nonetheless, several support groups exist and there are counselors and therapists who recognize the symptoms of PAS and can help women get over the condition.

> I went through, and still go through, severe mental problems—visualizing the procedure in my mind, hating myself, grieving and wanting to escape from the whole situation. No one ever told me about the emotional side effects after having an abortion.
>
> The abortion precipitated years of drug and alcohol abuse, an eating disorder and eventually a serious clinical depression. That supposedly safe procedure has had fourteen years of serious repercussions.

Depression can surface immediately after an abortion, or years and even decades later. A woman may be depressed, guilty, or angry. But PAS can be treated with the help of a professional counselor or therapist or by joining a support group like Women Exploited By Abortion (WEBA). WEBA's philosophy is that abortion is immoral, but a woman suffering from PAS does not have to arrive at the same conclusion in order to overcome her depression. What she needs is to work through her anger and accept her grief without bearing a burden of guilt. Even men involved in an abortion experience depression. One man wrote that he broke down and wept twenty years after his wife had an abortion.

EFFECT ON FUTURE PREGNANCIES

Though some researchers believe there is slightly higher risk of ectopic pregnancy (a pregnancy in which a fertilized egg implants in the Fallopian tube instead of the uterus) after abortion, they usually occur as a result of abortion only if a woman has had complications following her abortion. With abortions being done early in pregnancy and safer techniques being used, however, there is little proof that abortion has any effect on either future pregnancies or a woman's fertility.

No medical procedure is without risk, especially when spread over thousands of patients as indeed abortion is spread. But considering abortion's tragic history of medical complications and mortality, of back-alley butcher jobs and self-induced tragedies, clearly today's modern abortion services offer women the most medically safe abortions they have ever had available to them. And with recent developments like RU 486 on the horizon, the medical tragedies of the past are as remote as ever.

Chapter Four

THE ABORTION INDUSTRY

> I think the thing I will always remember most vividly . . . was walking up those three flights of darkened stairs and down that corridor . . . that dank hallway and the door at the end of it stay with me and chill my blood still.

Before abortion was legalized and services were widespread, finding someone to perform an abortion and gathering the funds to pay for it were monumental and, occasionally, insurmountable tasks. Each year, a few thousand women obtained therapeutic abortions in hospitals, but their number never reached ten thousand. Hundreds of thousands of women who sought abortions were compelled to seek out illegal, back-alley abortions, unless they were wealthy and well-connected.

> I was well into the second trimester before a friend in a distant city located an unlicensed M.D. to perform the abortion. It cost me $800.00 plus plane fare. Then, I earned about $225 per month.

An illegal abortion usually costs five hundred dollars and upwards and sometimes as much as seventeen hundred dollars. It must always be paid for in cash. If finding the cash proved formidable for many women, finding someone to perform the abortion proved no less so. Dr. Bernard Nathanson, author of *Aborting America*, and now a staunch antiabortion advocate, used to refer his wealthy patients to an abortionist practicing in Puerto Rico and later to one in London. When the London doctor arrived in the United States to perform abortions here, he charged $800 and did an average of six per day.

Between 1970 and 1973, a group of women ran an underground abortion clinic in Chicago called the "Jane clinic." They provided medically safe abortions to over eighteen hundred women at a cost of fifty dollars each.

But these examples were exceptions. For most women seeking an abortion, finding an abortionist was a hit or miss process that required making contact in an abortion "industry" that was little more than a loosely knit network shrouded in secrecy. It consisted of asking friends, relatives, or "colleagues" if they "knew someone who knew someone who knew someone who did abortions."

Because it was so difficult to procure an abortion and because time was not on a woman's side, she usually went to the first contact she was given, regardless of cost, location, or any other detail. Whether the abortionist had adequate medical training, sterile instruments, antibiotics, anesthesia, or even clean sheets was less a matter of how much the abortion cost or whom one knew and more a matter of luck. In the world of illegal abortion, there were no standards or regulations, just an abundance of horror stories.

Legalizing abortion changed everything. Even before the Supreme Court ruled on *Roe* v. *Wade*, when states like New York and California liberalized abor-

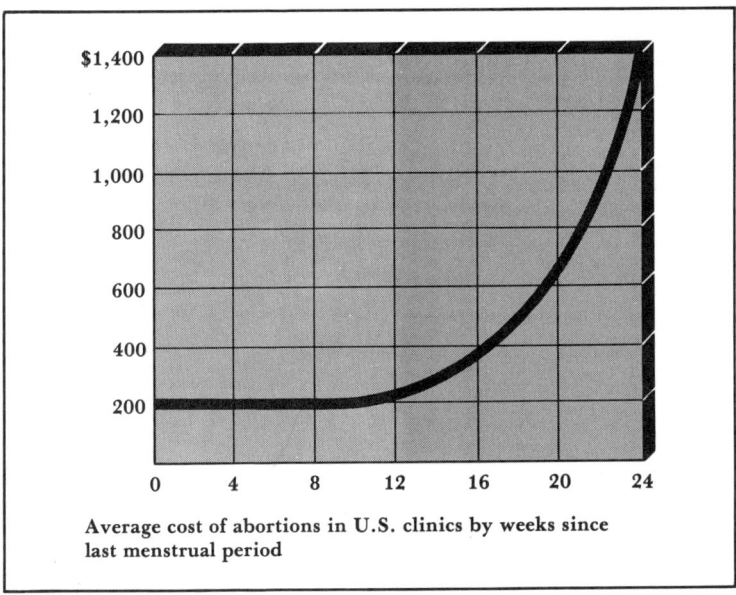

Average cost of abortions in U.S. clinics by weeks since last menstrual period

tion, clinics sprang up to meet the demand. In New York, between 1970 and 1973, there were over 150,000 legal abortions performed each year. Dr. Nathanson, who supervised the largest abortion clinic in the nation at the time, admits he was responsible for over sixty thousand abortions.

After *Roe* v. *Wade*, hospitals no longer had exclusive control of abortion services. Physicians were now permitted to do abortions in their private offices. In addition, independent, "free-standing" abortion clinics emerged that made abortion not only more available but also affordable. Compared to the exorbitant costs of illegal abortions in the past, the current cost of an abortion is nominal and has remained relatively stable despite inflation and a rise in health care costs. A first trimester abortion can be obtained for a few hundred dollars.

ABORTION FACILITIES

I feel fortunate that I could make the choice to have an abortion and do so without the fear of risking my life. I was able to go to a clean, legal medical facility and know that there would be a competent doctor to perform my abortion and that the staff would be able to give me good medical care. My doctor was excellent, the procedure was uncomfortable though not painful and I had no complications. However, had I had complications I would not have been abandoned in some back alley to fend for myself and probably die.

Today, women no longer have to settle for substandard places where their abortions are performed; clean, safe abortion facilities dot the United States. In the most recent survey of the industry, there were 2,680 abortion providers; 400 of these provided 60 percent of all abortions.[1]

One problem facing rural women is that most of the abortion facilities are located in urban areas. In 1985, only 32,000 abortions, or 2 percent of the total, were provided in rural communities or small towns.[2] Women who live in these non-metropolitan areas must travel to a facility. For some women, it is no problem, but for others, the distance and inaccessibility add expense to the abortion and create a hardship. In some cases, this actually deters women, particularly poor or young women, from having an abortion at all.

Most abortions are not performed in hospitals, but rather in "free-standing" clinics, which have no affiliation with a hospital. Although these clinics provide other services related to reproduction, such as sterilization, contraception, and pregnancy testing, their primary role is providing abortions. In 1985 they provided over 87 percent of all abortions. The remainder took place in hospitals or physicians' private offices.

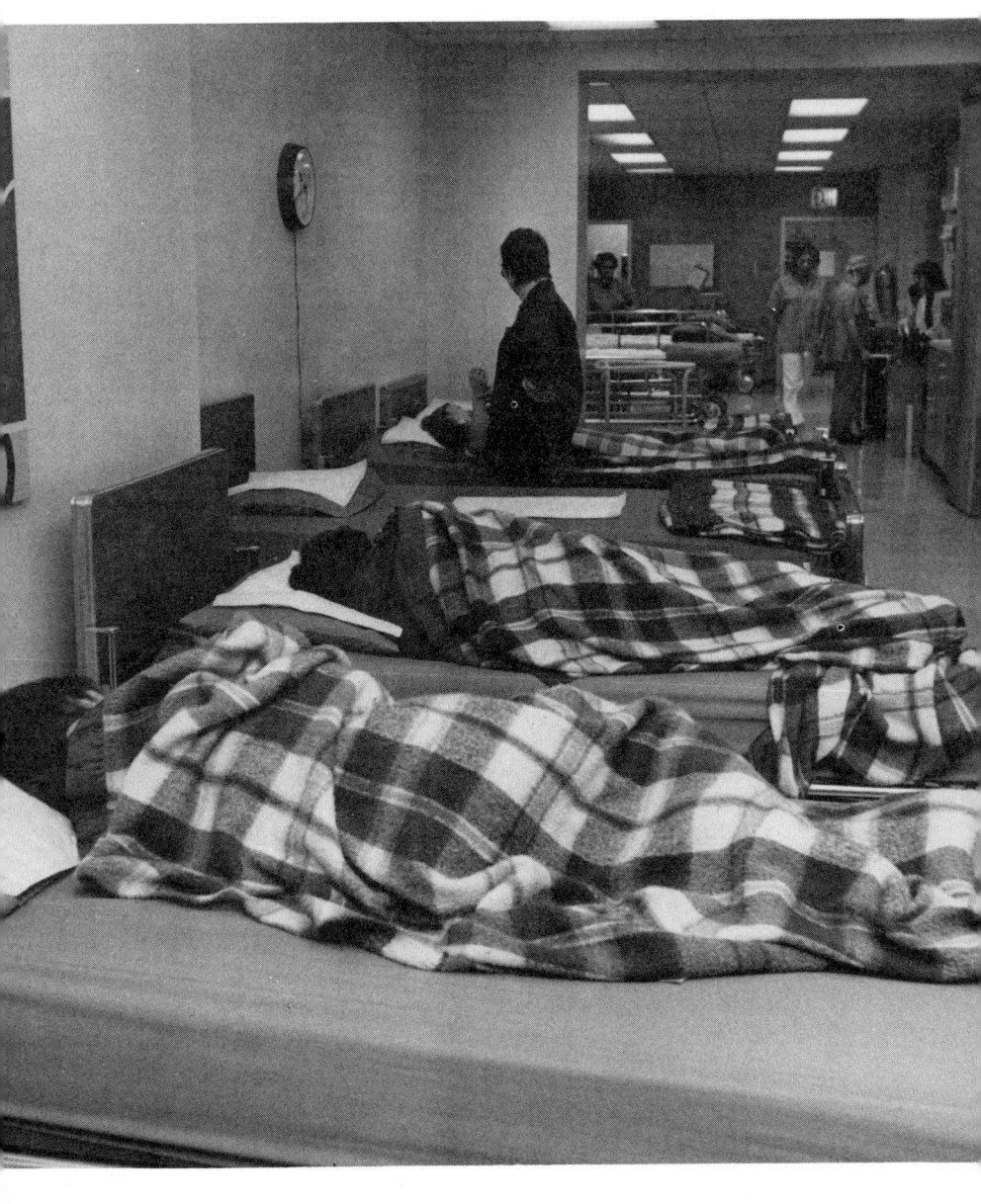

In the recovery room of an abortion clinic. The majority of abortions performed are done in clinics like this rather than in hospitals.

More and more clinics and hospitals, however, are reluctant to perform later abortions. Although 10 percent of all abortions occur after the first trimester, more than half of the abortion providers refuse to perform them.

There are several reasons that free-standing clinics have come to dominate the abortion industry. First is that they offer abortions at the most nominal cost. Charges for a first trimester abortion at a free-standing clinic range from $75 to nearly $900, but the average is around $200, compared to an average first trimester hospital abortion that costs over $700. Even mid-trimester abortions at clinics cost less; the average clinic mid-trimester abortion costs half that of the hospital mid-trimester abortion.[3] One of the reasons for the lower cost is that the physician performing an abortion in a clinic is not paid a private fee; the hospital physician collects a fee of several hundred dollars. Also, hospital abortions usually require an overnight stay in the hospital adding to the cost; clinic abortions are done as an out-patient service.

In addition to the lower cost of a clinic abortion, there are several other reasons for their domination of the abortion industry. Many private physicians are reluctant to perform abortions on their patients, and they refer them to the clinics. Also, it is much easier to get an appointment at a clinic. All a woman has to do is telephone the clinic. Phone numbers are listed in the *Yellow Pages* or advertised in the classified section of newspapers. In contrast, in a hospital, a woman normally must have a previously established professional relationship with a physician before an abortion can be performed there.

That many of these independent clinics are in business for a profit offends some people, even those supporting the right to have an abortion. But there is no distinction in the quality of services they provide compared to that of a hospital. In fact, many of the clinics offer more services, including pre-abortion counseling, contraception, gynecological care, screening and treatment for sexually transmitted diseases, male and female sterilization, and pre-natal and post-natal care.

Approximately half of all the independent clinics as well as some private physicians and a few hospital facilities belong to a professional organization called the National Abortion Federation, or NAF, which has developed and published industry standards. The NAF offers postgraduate courses for physicians and their staff, conducts research, and educates the public about the safety and availability of abortion services.

FINANCIAL AID FOR ABORTION

> You can get an abortion for a couple hundred dollars and that doesn't sound like a lot of money compared to what they used to cost before they were legal. But I'm young and single and don't have a couple hundred dollars to spare. If I needed an abortion, it would be difficult to come up with that much money.

Even before the Supreme Court legalized abortions, in those states which provided them, like New York and California, low-income women could get state funding for their abortions. Immediately following the Supreme Court's legalization of abortion, they were able to receive even more financial assistance from their private insurance plans or from both the state and federal governments. Low-income women who wanted abortions no longer had to scrounge up money from their families, friends, or even loan sharks, or take it from their meager savings or limited budgets. If a woman qualified for Medicaid, the government subsidized medical program for the indigent—and one-third of all the women who had abortions did qualify—then the government paid for her abortion. In 1977, the federal government paid ninety million dollars for approximately 300,000 abortions.[4]

In the United States, eleven million persons, mostly single women and children, live in poverty and receive federal aid.[5] In order to provide adequate medical service to them and to all other low-income individuals, Congress created the Medicaid program under Title XIX of the Social Security Act.

All but three states (Louisiana, Ohio, and Indiana) participated in this arrangement for abortion funding. Many individuals who were opposed to abortion, however, were outraged that their tax dollars were paying for abortions. One individual, Joseph Fahy, of Saraquoit, New York, conducted his own private protest against the Internal Revenue Service. Beginning in 1970, the year New York legalized abortion and began using Medicaid money to pay for it, Mr. Fahy withheld his income taxes as a form of protest, much the same way Henry David Thoreau had withheld his taxes over a century ago as a form of protest against war.

THE HYDE AMENDMENT

In Congress too, opponents of abortion searched for ways to alter the situation. During the 1976 Congressional session, Senator Henry J. Hyde, a staunch abortion foe, attached a rider to a huge Health, Education, and Welfare appropriations bill. Senator Hyde remarked that if he legally could, he would "prevent anybody from having an abortion, a rich woman, a middle-class woman, or a poor women." In its final form, the Hyde Amendment stated that no federal money could be used to fund abortion unless the life of the mother was endangered if the fetus were carried to term.

The appropriations bill was important because it included funding for many vital health, education, and welfare programs. Few congresspersons wanted to see it defeated. Therefore, although many did not want to support Senator Hyde's anti-abortion position, they still voted for the bill. It passed, and along with it, the Hyde Amendment rider.

Essentially, the Hyde Amendment gave a narrow definition of what was an acceptable abortion for the federal government to fund. Only those therapeutic abortions required to save the life of the mother could be funded by the federal government. The amendment excluded all elective abortions as well as any abortions that involved cases of rape or incest, or those needed to preserve the health of a woman. It is important to understand that at first the Hyde Amendment only affected *federal* money. It did not re-criminalize abortion or prevent any states from spending their own state Medicaid funds.

How could legislators justify voting for an amendment they opposed, even if they rationalized that it was a concession to a greater concern? The amendment dramatically affected many of the lives the larger bill was supposed to protect. If poor women couldn't get funding for their abortions, they might not be able to have abortions, and they would be faced with even more economic hardships. What many legislators reasoned, however, was that the Hyde Amendment was so restrictive, that even if it passed, the Supreme Court would strike it down later. This optimism, however, proved false.

The Hyde Amendment did have to wait until the Supreme Court litigated two cases, *Beal* v. *Doe* and *Maher* v. *Roe,* which concerned the funding of abortion. In a narrow, 5–4 decision, the Court supported the Hyde Amendment, and it went into effect. The court ruled that nowhere in the Constitution or the Social Security

Act was there evidence that any public tax money had to be spent on abortions. Not only did the federal government *not* have to pay for abortions (unless the woman's life was threatened), but now neither did the states. The decision was left up to the individual state legislatures.

Three years later, in 1980, the Supreme Court again addressed the issue of funding, and again firmly established its position on the Hyde Amendment. In *Harris* v. *McRae,* it reaffirmed that both the federal and the state governments could refuse to fund all but life-saving abortions without being in violation of the U.S. Constitution. According to the Court, *Roe* v. *Wade* protects a "negative" right, a right not to have the government interfere in privacy. It does not purport to protect a "positive" right, which would be the right to obtain an abortion, regardless of economic status.

That a woman cannot afford an abortion, the Court insisted, is not the fault of the government and does not fall under the guise of the decision. In his dissent of *Harris* v. *McRae,* Justice Blackmun, who had written the majority decision in *Roe* v. *Wade,* wrote that he was sure the states would "now accomplish indirectly what the Court had said they could not do directly. It is unrealistic," he continued, "to tell a poor woman she has the right to an abortion when she does not have the funds to pay for one."

There are those who believe that the government was shirking its responsibility by refusing to pay for women's abortions, arguing that everyone is entitled to decent health care. But Medicaid only purports to serve the *medical* needs of women, and all non-therapeutic abortions are not perceived as falling into the category Medicaid addresses. Supporters of the Hyde Amendment argue that non-therapeutic abortions are not a health care issue.

The Hyde Amendment did not apply solely to

Medicaid but, instead, to all federally funded medical programs. Thus, federal employees, Peace Corps volunteers, military personnel, and American Indians, all of whom depend on federally funded health care, were added to the numbers of welfare women also affected, bringing the total to over forty million women potentially restricted from receiving federal money to pay for an abortion.

Effects of the Hyde Amendment. When the Hyde Amendment went into effect in June 1977, federal funding of abortion came to an abrupt halt. Within two years, it decreased from ninety million dollars to less than a half million. The year Hyde was enacted, the federal government had paid for three hundred thousand abortions; a year later, it paid for less than five thousand, and by 1985, the number had dropped to less than five hundred.[6]

Individual states were no longer compelled to subsidize any but life-saving abortions, and many chose not to. Prior to the Hyde Amendment, only three states had refused to use their Medicaid funds, but since the amendment, thirty-seven refused.

Senator Hyde and his supporters had hoped that the amendment would curtail abortions. Because fourteen states and the District of Columbia still provide Medicaid funding for abortions, and five million low-income women live in those areas, 65 percent of all the low-income women who want abortions manage to get at least state-funded ones.

What happens to the remaining 35 percent? Most of them manage to find a way to pay for it themselves. Because they are already in financial straits, paying even two hundred dollars for an abortion poses a real hardship for most women. Often the money spent on the abortion would otherwise have gone for food, rent, utilities, and other essentials. Finding the money takes time. On the average, low-income women delay their abortions a few weeks while they scrape together the money. This delay, in turn, increases the risk of the abortion, and often advances the pregnancy to the point where the woman must have a different, more expensive procedure, adding hundreds of dollars to the initial cost. For some, the delay prevents them from having an abortion at all.

Since the Hyde Amendment went into effect, sixty to eighty thousand women every year cannot afford an abortion and carry their pregnancy to term. Several thousand others resort to illegal or self-induced abortions. And at what cost? According to the Center for Disease Control, in 1979, the restrictive funding due to the Hyde Amendment cost four women their lives.

Every year a total of a billion dollars is spent on abortions, a figure that, however large, represents less than 1 percent of all the money annually spent on health care.[7]

The government will pay for their childbirth expenses and even some of their medical expenses after the baby is born. It will pay for 90 percent of the sterilizations poor women get. An abortion can be obtained for a few hundred dollars, but for women who don't have that and can't get it from the government, their insurance, or even from their families or friends, it is too high a cost.

Chapter Five

WOMEN WHO OBTAIN ABORTIONS

I got pregnant when I was 14. I didn't even know I had engaged in "the" sexual act. I wasn't sophisticated or knowledgeable about sex. My parents finally realized I was pregnant and took me to the family doctor. He recommended that I have an abortion.

I had my abortion almost five years ago when I was 19 and my boyfriend was 22. That "boyfriend" and I are now married. I found out I was pregnant on a Saturday afternoon and had the abortion the following Tuesday morning. Who can make an important decision rationally like that in two days?

For every three women who get pregnant each year, one of them will choose to have an abortion. On the average, she will be young, white, and single. She probably uses birth control sometimes, but not always, and chances are, not the time she got pregnant. When she has an abortion, she is likely to be in her first trimester, and it will be done by vacuum aspiration. Chances are good that she will not suffer from any physical complications from her abortion. But "she" is only a composite, an average. Before citing statistics and averages, remember that each woman's story remains individual, unique, hers alone.

Worldwide, every year more than fifty million individual women, with fifty million individual stories, will have abortions. Listening to each story would be one way to understand abortion. But listening to all of them is impossible. Another way to understand abortion is to collect *statistical data,* which is the numbers of women who obtain abortions. Studying this information reveals why many women have abortions and how they were influenced by things like, for example, changes in the law or new developments in birth control.

Through surveys and reports, statisticians count the number of women each year who obtain an abortion. They divide these women into categories based on what they know about them, such as whether they are married, how old they are, their ethnicity, how many weeks their pregnancy had progressed at the time of abortion, what method was used. After this information has been collected, it is analyzed, studied, and used as the basis for other research on abortion. For instance, a statistician might study the number of teenage women having abortions to see how they are affected by changes in parental consent laws or sex education.

In the United States, two major organizations keep track of abortions: The Center for Disease Control (CDC), which is a branch of the United States government, and the Alan Guttmacher Institute (AGI), which is the research branch of Planned Parenthood. The CDC relies on state reports, while the AGI surveys all the facilities where abortions are performed. Its numbers are higher than the CDC's, but most researchers, including those at the CDC, consider the AGI figures to be the most accurate.

ABORTION WORLDWIDE

Three out of every four people in the world live in countries where abortion is legal, at least, to preserve a woman's health.[1] Half of these people live where an abortion can be obtained on demand. In nearly every industrialized nation, abortion is legal. Even in many countries where it is illegal, it is still widely practiced because the laws against it are not strictly enforced.

In the last two decades, particularly since 1980, the trend has been for countries to liberalize, rather than restrict, their abortion laws. The United States is one of the few industrialized nations where abortion is such a controversial topic.

Although most governments of the world encourage or at least tolerate abortion, one billion people, mostly from sub-Saharan Africa, Latin America, and the strongly religious fundamentalist Arab states, live in countries where women have no access to safe, legal abortion.

Naturally, illegal abortions go unreported, so it is impossible to count the exact number of women in the world who have abortions. Using surveys, mortality rates, and other sources of information, however, researchers have estimated that the number of women in the world who obtain abortions each year is between fifty and sixty million.[2] China, with fourteen million abortions performed, and the Soviet Union, with eleven million, lead the world figures.

Nations like China have high abortion rates because the government encourages its citizens to have small families; abortion is one method women use to reach that goal. In countries in Central and Eastern Europe, where reliable contraception is in short supply, abortion rates are high. Abortions there are usually obtained by married women trying to space their children or terminate childbearing. In contrast, in Western industrialized nations like the United States, the majority of abortions are obtained by young, unmarried women.

ANALYZING THE NUMBERS

Knowing how many women obtain abortions is interesting, but in order to study the information further in depth, researchers use two convenient statistical methods—*abortion rates* and *abortion ratios*. The type of information they learn from each method is different, but complementary.

The abortion rate and ratio are based only on women considered to be of "childbearing age," which statisticians define as 15–44 years old (even though some individuals are fertile before the age of fifteen, others beyond the age of forty-four, and some are not fertile at all).

The difference between a rate and ratio is the women who are counted. For the rate, all women of childbearing age are counted, while for the ratio only pregnant women are counted. Furthermore, a rate is always based on 1,000 women of childbearing age, but a ratio is either given for 1,000 or only 100 women, and sometimes, as a percentage. For example, the 1985 rate was 28, which means that for every 1,000 women in the United States aged 15–44, there were 28 who had an abortion. On the other hand, the 1985 ratio was 298, which means that for every 1,000 pregnant women, 298 terminated their pregnancy in an abortion.

What can statisticians learn from these numbers, beyond how many women are getting abortions each year? To begin with, they use the numbers to see if there is a trend in populations, either a drop in abortions or an increase from year to year. Thus, the 1985 rate of 28 can be compared to the 1973 rate of 16. Likewise, the ratio can also be used to compare one year to another. In 1985, the abortion ratio was almost

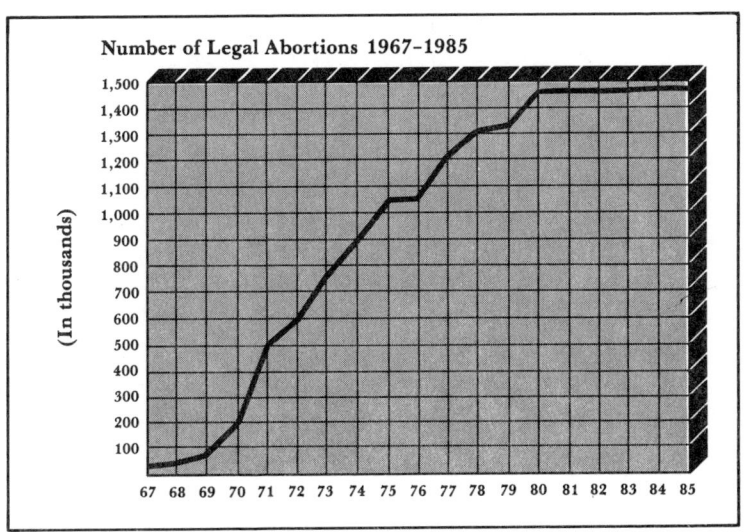

30 compared to the 1973 ratio which was 19. In the years between 1973 and 1985, 11 more pregnant women out of every 100 were likely to have an abortion.

Rates and ratios are also frequently used to compare one group of women to another group of women. For example, the most recent rate among teenagers (15–19) was 43 compared to older women (35–39), who had a rate of 10. To illustrate a comparison of ratios between groups, consider the 1983 ratio among white married women to white unmarried women. Married women had a ratio of seven compared to unmarried women whose ratio was 70, which meant that unmarried pregnant white women were 10 times more likely to terminate their pregnancy in abortion than those white women who were married.

Sometimes the total abortion rate is computed, which is the average number of abortions 1,000 women will have over their entire lifetime. In the Soviet Union, the total rate is 4,000, which means that the average Soviet woman is likely to have four abortions in her lifetime.

ABORTION IN THE UNITED STATES

There are approximately fifty-five million women of childbearing age in the United States and about one of every five has already had an abortion.[3] Every year six million women get pregnant, but slightly less than half of those pregnancies are intended. Of the 6.1 million who are pregnant, 3.7 million will have babies, 0.9 million will have a spontaneous abortion or miscarriage, and the remaining 1.6 million will have abortions.[4] Each year 3 percent of all the childbearing age women will have an abortion. On the average, three women will have an abortion every minute of the year.

After World War II, there were about a million illegal abortions each year.[5] Methods of birth control were available, but they were not as reliable as the pill or the intrauterine device, which gained in popularity during the 1960s. After women began using these more reliable methods, some researchers believe that they did not have as many abortions. Dr. Ray Adamek, a sociology professor at Kent State University, claims that in 1969, just before the first state legalized abortion, the total number of abortions could have been as low as 130,000. This low number is not merely attributable to women using more effective birth control. It probably also reflects the entire situation surrounding abortion: it was costly, risky, and difficult to obtain. Many women who would otherwise have had abortions entered "shotgun" marriages, placed their babies up for adoption, or became single parents.

In stark contrast to the number of illegal abortions, the number of legal abortions was rather small; eight thousand were reported in 1969. As states began to liberalize the abortion laws, the number of legal abortions rose dramatically. By 1973, the first year abortion was legalized nationally, almost three-quarters of a million

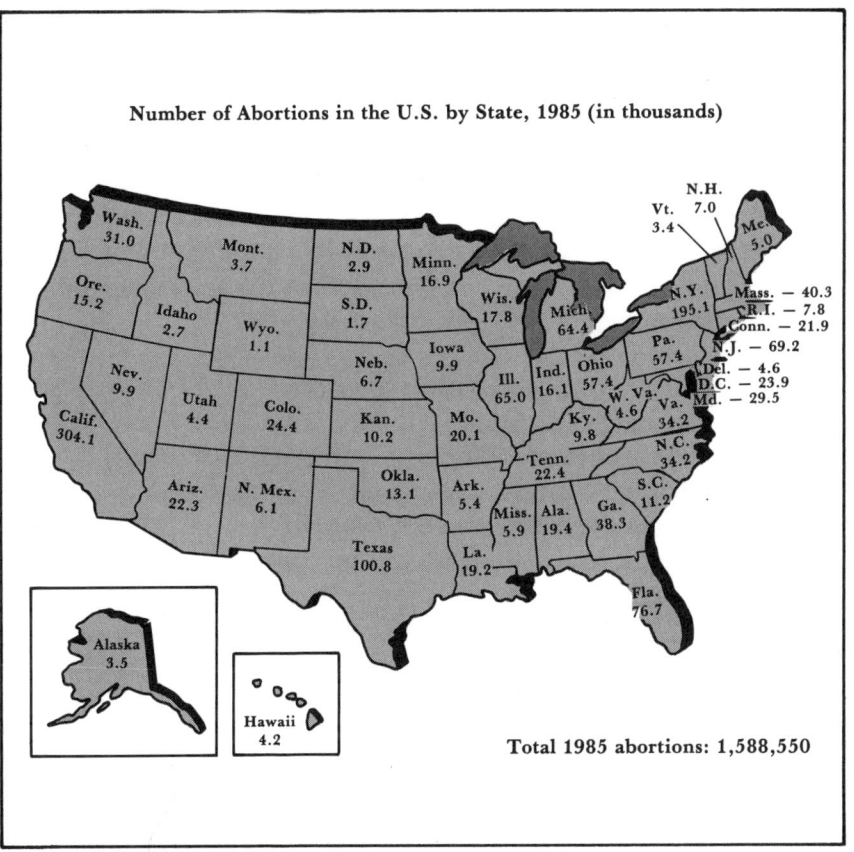

Number of Abortions in the U.S. by State, 1985 (in thousands)

Total 1985 abortions: 1,588,550

legal abortions were performed. After 1973, the number steadily climbed until it doubled; in recent years, it has declined slightly.

As the map indicates, abortion varies considerably from state to state, depending on the state's population, its abortion facilities, and even its abortion laws. For example, a state with strict parental consent laws might discourage women from having abortions as compared to a state with liberal laws.

STATISTICS ON ABORTIONS

In general, the majority of American women having abortions are young, single, and white. They have abortions by their twelfth week of pregnancy by vacuum aspiration. When they are pregnant, unmarried women, women over forty, teenagers, and non-white women, however, are the most likely to have an abortion; they have the highest abortion ratios.

Unplanned Pregnancy. Only 45 percent of all the pregnancies in a given year are planned; the rest are what researchers term "unintended pregnancy." In general, abortions are assumed to be the result of unintended pregnancies, though not all women with unintended pregnancies have abortions. About 0.4 million will miscarry and 1.3 million will give birth.[6]

Despite the availability of birth control, many couples fail to use it consistently and often find themselves facing an unplanned pregnancy. In a survey conducted by *People* magazine, only 39 percent of the high school and 58 percent of the college students surveyed reported using birth control each time they had sex. Another study by the Alan Guttmacher Institute revealed that an estimated three million sexually active women use no birth control at all, and many more fail to use it each time they engage in sexual intercourse.

Every time a fertile woman has sex without using contraception, she has a 4 percent chance of getting pregnant. Over the course of a year, four out of every five sexually active females playing contraceptive roulette will find themselves pregnant. Tragically, many victims of rape or incest are included in the tally (2–4 percent of all victims become pregnant). Researchers estimate that half of all abortions could be avoided if couples used contraception consistently, and even more if they used highly reliable methods like the pill.[7]

Abstinence is one way to ensure not getting pregnant; so is sterilization. But abstinence is not a choice for many women, while sterilization is inappropriate for those who want children in the future. No birth control method guarantees a women complete freedom from pregnancy. Some methods are more reliable than others, but, in general, because methods do fail or people fail to use them correctly, 15 percent of all women will get pregnant despite the use of contraception. One-fourth to half of all abortions are performed on women whose birth control has failed.[8]

Age. Although young women have the most number of abortions, they also have the most number of pregnancies and are actually less likely than older women to have an abortion rather than give birth. In fact, women aged 25–29 are the least likely of all childbearing-age women to have an abortion when they find themselves pregnant. Only 22 percent of pregnant women in that age group have abortions, compared to women over forty, who are the least likely to get pregnant but the most likely to terminate a pregnancy. One half of women over forty have an abortion when they are pregnant.[9]

Teenagers have the highest abortion ratio; 43 percent of their pregnancies end in abortion.[10] American teens get pregnant more than teenagers in most other developed nations. They have more babies and more abortions. More than one million teens get pregnant each year, and approximately one out of every twenty eighteen and nineteen year olds will have an abortion.

Marital Status. The majority of abortions are performed on single women. Among teenagers having abortions, 96 percent are unmarried.[11] The most recent figures (1985) indicate that four out of every five abortions are performed on unmarried women. In addition, 5 percent of all childbearing-aged single women

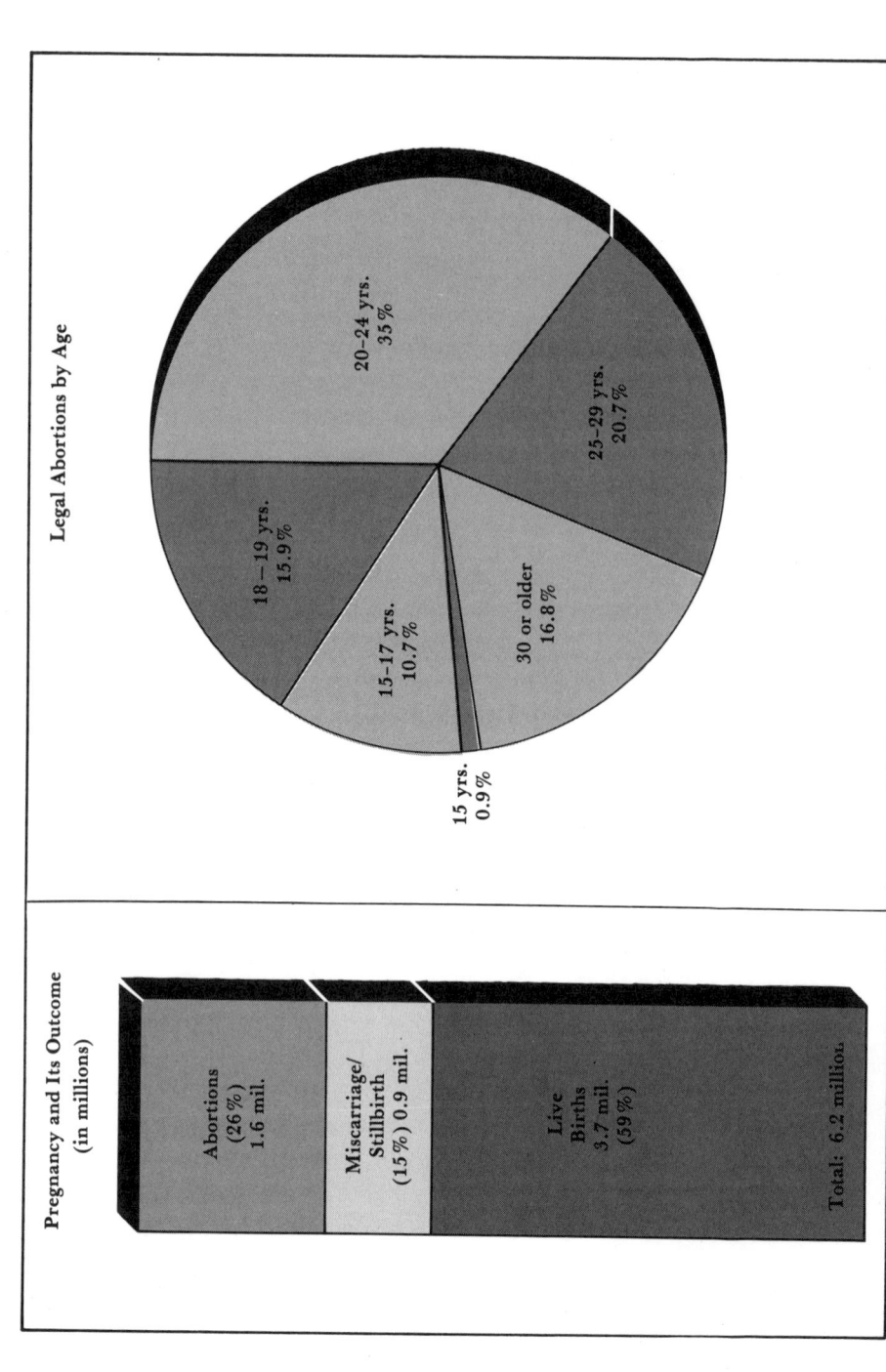

will have an abortion, compared to 1 percent of all childbearing married women.

Single women have almost twice as many abortions as births, while married women have almost ten times as many births as abortions. The difficulty of raising a child without a partner is one reason, but today more and more single women are postponing childbearing or scheduling their pregnancies to accommodate their education and careers. Married women, despite the pursuit of an education or career, have more social pressure not to terminate a pregnancy by abortion. As expected, they get pregnant more frequently, have more babies, and resort to abortion less than their single sisters.

Previous Abortions. Before abortion was legal, most women were reluctant to say they had had an abortion, so it is difficult to accurately determine exactly how many women are having abortions for the first time. Since 1973 though, researchers believe that the number of women who have an abortion a second, third, and even fourth time has increased substantially. Contributing to the increase is the accumulation of years since abortion was legalized, but it is also the willingness of women to disclose previous abortions.

Gestation. As mentioned in a previous chapter, half of all abortions are performed by the first six weeks of conception; 91 percent or 1.4 million, by the first twelve weeks. Another 140,000 are performed during the fourth and fifth months and 12,000 during the sixth month or later.[12]

Getting the money to pay for the abortion, having to go to court to bypass parental consent requirements, or experiencing difficulty finding an abortion facility, all contribute to delays in abortions. For teens, particularly the younger ones, the delay is often the result of not realizing they are pregnant.

MORTALITY

Historically, gruesome stories of abortion mortality abound. Estimates of the number of deaths prior to *Roe* v. *Wade* vary, but during the two decades preceding the legalization of abortion, the estimates were between 200–500 a year.[13] Today, with safer procedures available as well as earlier abortions and more physicians who are more skilled at the procedure, the mortality statistics have decreased dramatically. (Thus, for every 250,000 abortions performed, there is likely to be one death.)

Statistics can have a chilling effect on the issue of abortion. Though each woman's story remains hers alone, when millions of abortions are counted, the numbers are dramatic. For what the numbers reveal are sweeping changes in the status and sexual freedom of women and increasing tolerance and widespread acceptance of abortion. These facts are disturbing to some and reassuring to others. Furthermore, the statistics on abortion prove that despite the continuing controversy, thousands of women have abortions every day of every year.

Chapter Six

THE WAY PEOPLE FEEL ABOUT ABORTION

> I had an abortion eleven years ago. It was, without a doubt, the worst experience of my life. Because of my abortion I stand and say abortion is wrong!
>
> I am speaking out now because we cannot return to that time of terror for all women. A time when women had to risk their lives in order to have some control of their lives. Women have chosen abortion since the beginning of time and will continue to do so; we must maintain it as a safe, legal option for all women.

Abortion is one of the most controversial issues in the United States. It has been the focus of many political campaigns. There is so much spirited argument going on between the abortion opponents and supporters that it appears they are evenly divided on the issue. On one side are the "right to lifers," ready to amend the Constitution, close down every clinic, and persuade every woman contemplating abortion not to have one. On the other side are pro-choice advocates insisting it is every woman's right to have an abortion. Two camps of people diametrically opposed.

Public opinion polls suggest a different story, however. Fewer than 20 percent of Americans polled believe abortion is always morally wrong, regardless of the reason; 20–25 percent believe a woman is entitled to an abortion if she wants one.[1] Although there is a wide gulf between these staunch opinions, what lies between them is not a vacuum, but the majority of Americans who believe abortion should be legal, at least for compelling reasons. How to define a compelling reason, however, remains in question.

PUBLIC ATTITUDES

Most Americans support the right to have an abortion for "hard," compelling reasons: to save the mother's life, if her health is seriously threatened; if she is a victim of rape or incest; or if her fetus is grossly deformed. Fewer Americans support abortion for the "soft" reasons: if a woman is single, young, poor, or the timing of the pregnancy is inconvenient.

Whether or not some people believe abortion is acceptable depends not only on the circumstances but also on the development of the fetus. They are more inclined to support the right to an early, first-trimester abortion than a second trimester, or especially, a third trimester one.

People who believe abortion is moral think it should be legal, but not all people who believe it is immoral are willing to make abortion illegal. According to one study, only 47 percent of those interviewed who believed abortion is immoral wanted it to be illegal.[2]

Although the majority of Americans feel abortion, at least for a "hard" reason, is moral, they are not necessarily willing to support it with their tax dollars, especially for women obtaining abortions for "soft" rea-

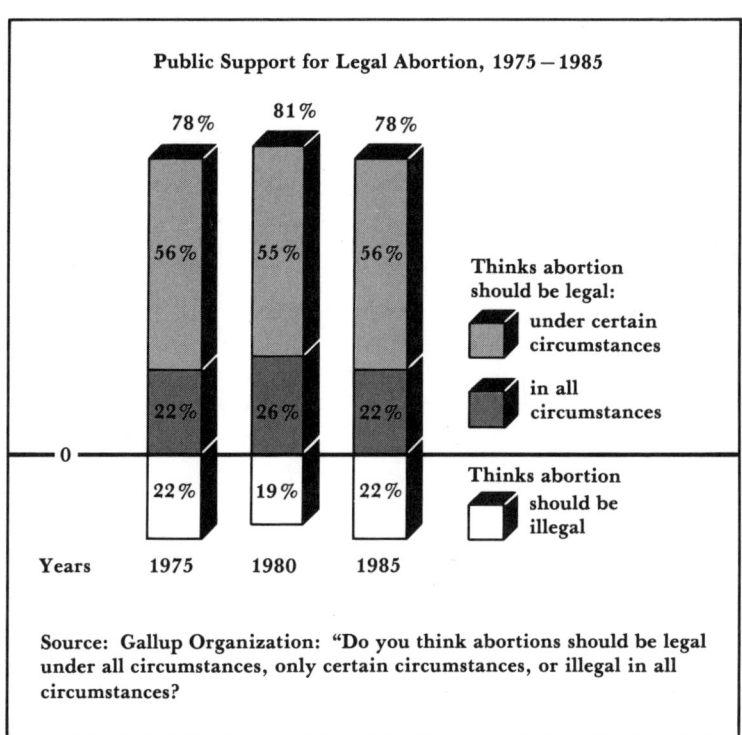

sons. In an ABC/*Washington Post* poll (1981), about half of the people did not feel that the government should have to pay for a woman's abortion.

Factors Influencing Attitudes. Many factors influence the way people feel about abortion: their religious beliefs, whether or not they have had an abortion or know someone who has had one, where they live, their education, their income, and their life style. While generalizations about groups of people can be drawn from the polls, it is important not to assume that any individual in one of these groups would feel the same way. To do so would be to stereotype people with regard to their views on abortion.

In general, Conservative and Reform Jews have the most liberal views towards abortion (Orthodox Jews believe abortion is immoral), while Catholics have the least tolerant views. In one poll that asked if "abortion should be a private decision between a woman and her physician without government interference," 98 percent of the Jews polled felt that it should be, compared to 86 percent of the Protestants and 75 percent of the Catholics.[3]

Despite their differences, however, Catholics and Protestants report the same percentage of abortions.

The more education an individual has completed, the more likely he or she is to support abortion, and high school appears to be a crucial factor. Those who have dropped out of high school are far more likely to condemn abortion than those who have completed high school, college, or graduate school.

Because a person's income is often directly related to the amount of education he or she has, and education was a factor in a person's views of abortion, the more income a person has, particularly a woman, the more tolerant of the right to abortion she is likely to be.

Residents of large cities are more likely to support the right to have an abortion than residents of small cities or rural areas, and people living on either the East or West coasts are more likely to support the right to have an abortion than those living in the Midwest or the South.

Perhaps because abortion has been legal and accessible during most of their lifetimes, younger people are more likely to support the right to have an abortion. Interestingly, some poll results indicated that the men who were polled were more likely to have a liberal view towards abortion than women, although it must be remembered that millions of men don't.[4]

Although the differences are narrowing, in the past,

white people have been more tolerant of abortion than blacks. Historically, the black sector of the community viewed abortion as a "conspiracy" to keep their population from increasing. Abortion was commonly referred to as "race genocide." Moreover, since blacks have been far more tolerant of single parenthood than whites, they were less likely to see abortion as a way to deal with illegitimacy. White middle and upper class teenagers, however, tend to see abortion as a way to deal with out-of-wedlock pregnancies.

An individual is more likely to support the right to have an abortion if those close to him or her also support it. For example, a daughter is more likely to support the right to have an abortion if her mother does also; a husband if his wife does; a woman if her friends do.

PERSONAL ATTITUDES

In 1977 I became pregnant while using an I.U.D. for birth control. The man wanted no part of a baby and ultimately no part of myself.

When the doctor told me I was pregnant, a feeling of despair flooded my body. Ever since I was a young girl I had dreamed about having a baby. I would lie in bed at night with a pillow on my stomach fantasizing I was carrying a child. Only, my fantasy involved a loving husband who like myself wanted a family life. The reality was far from that. It was very sad for me; finding out I was pregnant was the worst thing that happened to me. That's not how it's supposed to be. Still, my first thoughts were not to have an abortion. Maybe things would work out, somehow the fantasy would evolve. It didn't.

As for adoption, I very much respect those women having gone that route. It is truly a self-

> less act of love. But for myself, I knew that if I was to have the baby, I would want to keep it. Envisioning what my life would be, an unskilled, unwed mother . . . that's not the life I wanted to give my child and not what I wanted for myself.
>
> Also, I thought about being emotionally tied to this man, through our child, and what a sad father he would be. It started to become clear that I didn't want to have this child. By the time I went for counseling, I had decided to abort.

How a woman feels about abortion depends on many factors, the same ones that influence the results in the public opinion polls. Not all women who have had an abortion support it.

In one study (Matire and Henshaw), researchers found that one-fourth of the women who had abortions felt that it was morally wrong; 8 percent of them did not believe that any woman who wants an abortion should be able to obtain it legally.

Probably the most important influence on a woman's attitude towards abortion is when she is faced with her own unplanned pregnancy. Being pregnant can change a woman's opinion about abortion. It is not unusual for a woman who had supported abortion, perhaps even had one previously, to change her mind about it. One woman who had an experience with abortion and became pregnant again two years later said,

> I decided that this time I was not going to put myself through that horrible pain. I decided to keep my baby. At the time I had my abortion, an untimely birth seemed far worse than an abortion. Unfortunately, I was wrong.
>
> Since my abortion, I have not regretted keeping this baby. She is more of a blessing than

> I had imagined. Life is not easy being a single parent, but I have been blessed with the happiness of having my baby. Then [the abortion] I had sacrificed a tiny life for my freedom and paid dearly with my freedom.... I lost my baby, my boyfriend, my job, my dignity, and almost my life. Now I have a new life with my daughter. Each time I look at her, I am grateful for having made the right choice.

Some women who had been opposed to abortion, perhaps even to the point of actively working to stop it, may find themselves pregnant and desperate for an abortion. One professional, working at an Akron, Ohio abortion clinic that had been the target of much anti-abortion protest, reported that two of the women who had picketed the clinic on a regular basis came in for abortions. "I always felt abortion was wrong until I found myself in this situation," one of the women told her. In one study of abortion protesters who later have abortions, one woman surveyed rationalized her new position by claiming that it was somehow "different" than other women's.

Most often, a woman's attitude about abortion reflects not only her values and lifestyle, but more importantly, the circumstances she faces at the time she is pregnant.

> Even though I am a Family Planning Professional, and with all my knowledge of family planning, I was like any other woman who had an unintended pregnancy. I was terrified and felt as though my life was out of control.

For most women, making the decision to have an abortion is not easy or trivial, as some critics have suggested. In her study of the way women make these decisions, Carol Gilligan concluded that the decision to abort is rarely a selfish decision. More typically, a woman arrives at her decision by considering the other significant people in her life and the effect that either bearing a child or having an abortion will have on them.

A key issue, women report, is how exploited and hurt they often feel, especially if they have been abandoned by the father. Faced with an unwanted pregnancy, many women choose abortion as the least terrible of a variety of hurts; their decision to abort usually entails picking the lesser of two evils.

> It [abortion] was not easy for me or my family when I was young. It will never be something women do without feeling that it is the last, but probably most necessary, option they would consider.

ATTITUDES OF FATHERS

> I have never felt such grief and sorrow. I have never had to face a choice so difficult. I am joyful that my daughter was set free from the hardships of being human without ever having been a normal or an independent adult [about the Down's syndrome fetus his wife aborted]. I am also grieving that I never raised her and shared in wonderful life experiences with her.

Women are not the only people affected by abortions. Although some men abandon women or are excluded from the decision and the experience itself, many are part of the decision about abortion. They sit in the waiting room; they deal with the aftermath. Like many women having abortions, when the procedure is over, many men report a sense of relief. But ambivalent feelings and grief can linger long after the abortion.

> I've pretty much put the abortion in the back of my mind, but it's still there. As a matter of course, I try to think good thoughts instead of bad thoughts, and I get away with it most of the time. But the bad ones creep up on you. The abortion itself was probably the least of all the problems. But it's the situation around it that makes you really think how you feel about the lady. This is life-and-death stuff.

For many couples, the pregnancy and the abortion become a part of their history together, a time they shared.

> I was involved in the conception. I was involved in the decision to terminate. I've been involved in the feelings, and I want to be involved in the resolution. That's the way our life is.

Others are not so positive; abortion can disrupt and even break up a relationship. Men who oppose abortion are often helpless to prevent it.

> The abortion was her idea. I don't believe in it. Period. I would rather that she had had the baby, but she's the one who's got to contain it; she's the one who's got to go through all the trouble, so she said she wanted the abortion and I went along with it.[5]

When a woman is counseled on abortion, the emphasis is placed on her to make a decision with which she can live. Although some young girls may include their parents, or at least their mother in the decision, many young girls do not. Some parents are extremely supportive of their daughter's decision; other parents are not so grateful. Abortion may go against their own moral views. Often, they are as shocked and outraged to discover their daughter was having sex, as they are that she is pregnant.

ATTITUDES OF PHYSICIANS

Until women have safe, efficient methods to self-induce their own abortions, their right to privacy, as sociologist Jonathan Imber notes in his book, *Third Parties in Abortion Decisions,* depends on a physician's willingness to do abortions. The Supreme Court protected a woman's right to have an abortion, but in a later decision, it also protected the doctor's right not to perform one.

Imber studied twenty-six obstetrician/gynecologists in a small city that had no free-standing abortion clinic. He found that only a third of the physicians were willing to perform an abortion and only two would perform one after 12 weeks gestation.

He also found a lot of professional ambivalence towards doing abortions. Doctors were torn between their conviction that a woman has the right to an abortion and their own willingness to perform the procedure. Some of the physicians refused to perform abortions because doing so ran counter to their personal beliefs on the issue; others found abortions clinically uninteresting; still others did not want to become known in their community as the "local abortionist."

Most abortion clinics rely heavily on resident physicians to perform the abortions, largely because once most physicians complete their residency and set up their own practice, they no longer have to rely on doing abortions to subsidize their incomes. In addition, many physicians find second trimester and especially third trimester abortions emotionally draining and try to avoid them, especially if there is the possibility of delivering a live fetus.

Though most of the physicians in Imber's study were reluctant to perform abortions, especially later abortions, in a recent survey of the members of the American College of Obstetricians and Gynecologists, it was reported that female physicians were more likely than male physicians to support a woman's right to have an abortion under specific circumstances. Perhaps as more women enter this specialty of medicine, there will be more physicians in private practice who are willing to perform abortions.

Public opinion polls only reflect how people feel about the issue. What the polls cannot predict is whether abortion will be tolerated ten, fifty, or a hundred years from now. As history teaches, times change, and usually with change comes new perspectives and new opinions about what is acceptable and what is not.

Today, it is often taken for granted that anyone who supports population control, especially those who are concerned about the world population explosion, will have a liberal attitude towards abortion. Planned Parenthood, an international family planning organization, frequently counsels women about their right to have an abortion. In fact, there is quite a controversy over their use of public funds in light of this service they provide. Ironically, however, Margaret Sanger, one of the founders of Planned Parenthood and an early birth control advocate, reflected an attitude towards abortion that was remarkably similar to the right-to-life position today. For Sanger, abortion was a "savage" method of fertility control.

Chapter Seven

THE POLITICS OF ABORTION

Abortion is a complex political issue affecting millions of women. Until the 1960s, its political history was largely connected to the medical community, but since then it has become a broad political issue, influencing public policy as never before.

Though thousands of women demonstrated for the liberalization and repeal of abortion laws during the 1960s, it was only when the Supreme Court ruled on *Roe* v. *Wade* in 1973 that unprecedented numbers of people entered the pro-life political arena. The Supreme Court's decision was more liberal and so counter to traditional Christian doctrine that it caught many by surprise and stirred their outrage, compelling them to do something to stop abortion.

Determined not to lose the ground they had gained, pro-choice women continue to voice their concern about keeping abortion legal.

PRO-CHOICE GROUPS

Women will never willingly return to the horrors and injustices of illegal abortions again. We

will be silent no more—those of us who can afford the painful price. Your mothers, wives, daughters, friends and relatives, millions of us are among the silent who cannot come forward with their truth. Those of us who can, carry their burden and insist that abortion must remain legal, safe and accessible to avoid another millennium of agony and peril.

Like the original movement to reform abortion, the twentieth century campaign to repeal abortion laws was largely instigated by physicians. During the 1960s, they were joined by thousands of women involved in the equal rights movement, women who saw reproduction freedom as an important element in equality, particularly economic equality. In addition, they were joined by members of both religious and secular groups.

In 1969, the first single issue group dedicated to the repeal of the abortion issues was founded. Called the National Association for the Repeal of Abortion Laws and later renamed the National Abortion Rights Action League (NARAL), it has been one of the most influential organizations in the movement and remains the largest and most formidable pro-choice organization, claiming more than 150,000 members nationwide.

Other groups like the National Organization for Women (NOW), the Ms. Foundation, and the Women's Political Caucus have included the abortion issue as a

A pro-abortion rally. Pro-choice individuals believe a woman should have reproductive freedom and that it should be a woman's right to determine for herself whether or not to have an abortion.

major part of their agendas, while smaller groups such as the Boston Women's Health Collective also contribute, advocating a woman's right to abortion as one way to control her reproduction.

Liberal religious groups, predominantly from established Protestant and Reformed Jewish congregations, banded together to form the Religious Coalition for Abortion Rights, a national organization comprised of more than 30 groups advocating the right to choose abortion. There is also a liberal faction within the Catholic Church, called Catholics for Free Choice, which defends a woman's right to have an abortion and convenes for an annual convention, providing a forum for the topic.

The Reproductive Freedom Project, a branch of the American Civil Liberties Union, has provided much of the legal counsel for abortion cases that have succeeded *Roe* v. *Wade*. Another group, Planned Parenthood Federation of America, participates in the mainstream of abortion politics. Its research branch, the Alan Guttmacher Institute (AGI), is one of the major resource centers for statistical data on abortion. Under its guise, it publishes *Family Planning Perspectives,* one of the leading journals publishing abortion studies.

Although abortion is not their main focus, dozens of other organizations encompassing diverse interests support legal abortion. These groups range from the American Association of University Women, the League of Women Voters, and the Junior League to the National Conference of Black Lawyers, the Sierra Club, and the American Veterans Committee.

RIGHT-TO-LIFE GROUPS

I cannot commend too highly the dedication of citizens like you who have worked, struggled, and prayed for years to save the unborn and to give

crucial help to their mothers. You have helped make your fellow-citizens understand that abortions kill babies and that positive alternatives are available. . . . Because of your selfless efforts, I am confident that we shall prevail in restoring legal protection of the right to life to all Americans.
—Ronald Reagan (January 7, 1987)

Unlike the pro-choice movement, the pro-life movement has had minimal support from physicians and feminists: most of its members come from religious organizations. Though other religious groups, such as the Mormons, Southern Baptists, and American Orthodox Jews oppose abortion, it is the Roman Catholic Church that has been most politically influential in abortion politics. Not until the most recent movement to reform and repeal abortion laws, which culminated in the Supreme Court's *Roe* v. *Wade* decision, however, has the pro-life movement, including the Catholic Church, been so politically involved in the issue.

The Catholic Church formed a Bishop's committee to deal with all issues they perceived to affect the value of life, issues that included not only abortion, but also the environment and nuclear disarmament. Taking their initiative from the Bishop's committee, many members of the Catholic Church who were concerned about the *Roe* v. *Wade* decision founded an organization called the National Right-to-Life Committee (NRL) in June 1973. The National Right-to-Life Committee is a single-issue group focused on putting an end to legal abortion. Though it still maintains a largely Catholic constituency, the NRL embraces others, mainly fundamental and Evangelical Christians who share its cause. It remains one of the most influential pro-life organizations, with over 2,500 chapters spanning all fifty states. One of the most effective statewide Right-to-Life committees is located in Cincinnati, Ohio, and is chaired by Dr. J. C. Wilkie, author of *Handbook on Abortion,* the "abortion bible," a book summarizing pro-life's arguments.

Other groups opposed to abortion include Catholics United for Life (CUL), which is best known for starting "sidewalk counseling"; the American Life League, an orthodox Catholic group also opposed to birth control; and Birthright, a national network of crisis pregnancy counseling centers offering alternatives to abortion. Several multi-issue groups like the National Youth Pro-Life Coalition, the Eagle Forum, Concerned Women of America, and the Moral Majority also oppose abortion. Women Exploited by Abortion (WEBA) was founded to help women suffering from Post Abortion Syndrome.

A trend in recent years has been for members of the pro-life movement to form alliances with members of the disabilities rights movement. Aborting a genetically "defective" fetus is one of the most publicly acceptable reasons to have an abortion. But sentiment among pro-life people is that the struggle to protect fetuses is akin to the struggle of the disabled to gain status and respect and be valued in our society.

SEPARATION OF CHURCH AND STATE

History of Abortion in the Catholic Church. Theologians with the Roman Catholic Church have debated abortion throughout its two thousand year history. While it has always been considered a sin if used to cover-up a sexual act such as adultery, fornication, or anything outside the conjugal union, it has not always been considered homicide from the moment of conception. In fact, through much of its history, the official position, as first set down by Gratian in 1140 in the first Code of

Canon Law, was that abortion was homicide only after the fetus became a "formed" human being, which is the moment it acquires a soul, called hominization.[1] For many centuries, hominization was believed to occur after 40 days in a male fetus and after 80 days in a female fetus, although how the gender was determined is unknown.

Then in 1588, Pope Sixtus V, trying to control prostitution and other illicit sex in Rome, issued the bull, *Effraenatum,* in which he stated that abortion at any time during the pregnancy was homicide, both a moral sin and a secular crime.[2] He abolished the 40–80 day hominization belief in favor of the idea that hominization began at conception. Only three years later, in 1591, after Sixtus had died, Pope Gregory XIV issued *Sedes apostolica,* tempering Sixtus's position by stating that "where no homicide or animated fetus is involved, not to punish more strictly than the sacred canons or civil legislation does."[3] Thus, the idea of abortion being less serious before hominization (40–80 days, not at conception) was reestablished and prevailed until 1864, when the theologian Jean Gury decided that hominization is an irrelevant basis for abortion. In Gury's opinion, all abortions involved a potential human being, and, therefore, were all immoral. This idea gained support, and in 1869, Pope Pius IX published *Apostolicae sedis,* in which he too bypassed the question of ensoulment, recommending excommunication for all who had abortions, including therapeutic ones.[4] This view has persisted until today.

The most recent development of official church position on abortion has been to condemn abortion on the grounds that what begins as human life (and not necessarily a full human being) is morally entitled to the "right to life." In 1968, Pope Paul VI explained this position, declaring a concern for human life that demands that abortions, therapeutic or otherwise, be prohibited, a position continually reaffirmed by his successors.

While some Catholic theologians have argued in favor of therapeutic abortions, the official position of the church is that all abortions be condemned. Only a medical procedure that indirectly takes the life of a fetus, such as the life-saving surgery for an ectopic pregnancy in which the Fallopian tube is removed, indirectly killing the fetus growing inside it, is sanctioned. Any procedure that directly takes the life of the fetus, on the other hand, is immoral.

Separation of Church and State. Although other churches like the Southern Baptist and the Mormon Church have been actively involved in the abortion issue, it is because the Roman Catholic Church has contributed so much money and taken such an active stand against abortion that it has been the target of accusations about jeopardizing the separation between church and state.

Legislation is supposed to neither favor nor penalize religion. But when there is a lack of agreement about what is moral, as in the abortion issue, it is impossible to create legislation that can possibly satisfy all the divergent religious views.

A church may advocate a moral stand, but it may not direct social policy that goes against people who do

The Catholic Church in the U.S. has an enormous influence on the abortion question. As these photographs indicate, however, there is dissent from traditional Catholic doctrine even within the church.

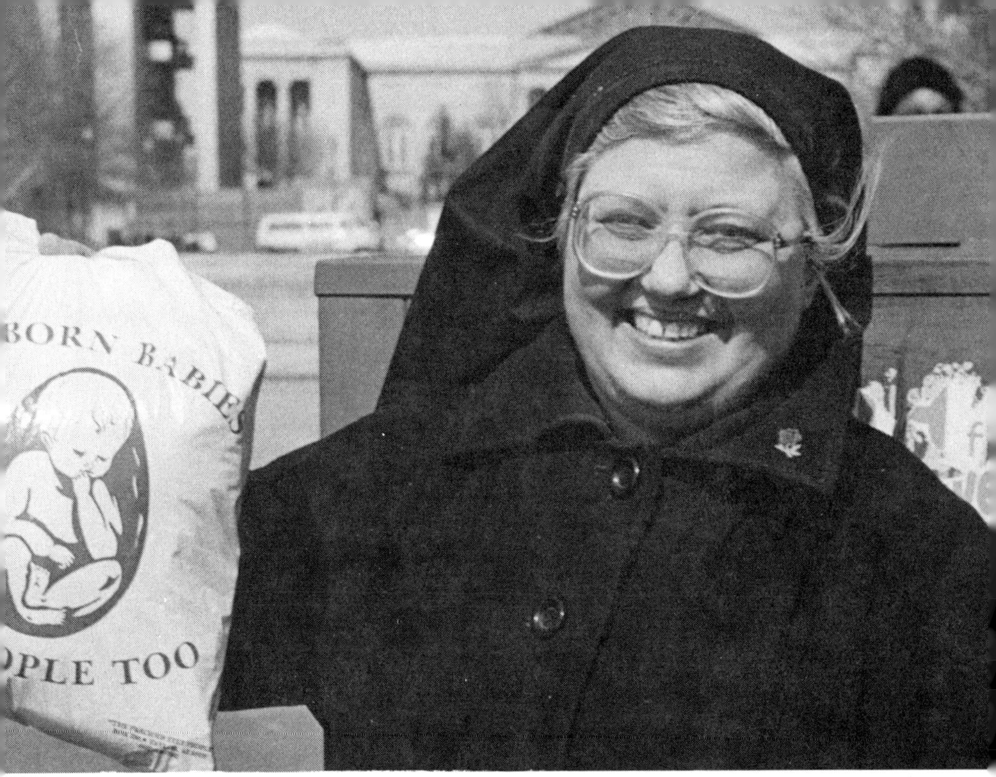
BORN BABIES
PLE TOO

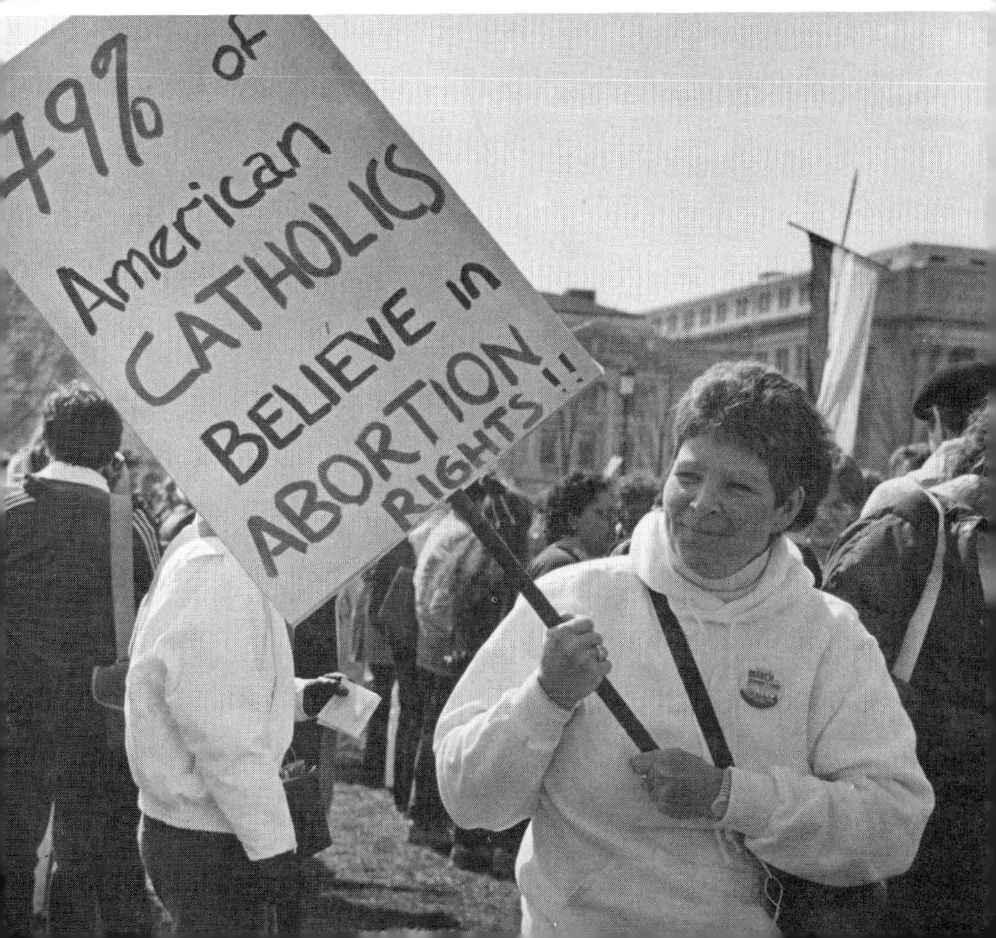
79% of
American
CATHOLICS
BELIEVE in
ABORTION
RIGHTS!!

not share that particular morality. What clouds this issue is whether indeed abortion is a public issue, as the Roman Catholic Church charges, or whether it is a private moral issue, as the Supreme Court decided. What the church perceives as a moral issue and within the scope of the law is frequently dismissed by others as a "religious" issue, outside the scope of the law.

Thus, while the Catholic Church is certainly guaranteed the right to persuade its fifty million members not to have abortions or support the right to have one, whether it should also be allowed to deny others that right through its political influence is a key issue. The Free Exercise clause of the First Amendment guarantees absolute freedom to hold religious beliefs and opinions, but the freedom to act, even in accordance with a religious belief, is not totally free from legislative restrictions.

A central facet of the debate over the separation of church and state is what limits ought to be placed on the involvement of a non-profit religious organization like the Catholic Church in directly shaping public policy and legislation. Because churches are charitable organizations that "do good," as a matter of legislative grace, they are not required to pay taxes and donations to them are not taxable. If a non-profit, tax-exempt organization tries to influence legislation or acts like a political interest group by lobbying legislators or contributing to candidates' election funds, then the courts can revoke its tax-exempt status. In 1974, the Women's Lobby sued the National Conference of Catholic Bishops (NCCB) for failure to register as a lobby under the Federal Lobbying Act. The NCCB did not deny the charges and registered as a political action committee (PAC) under the name National Committee for a Human Life Amendment.

The next year, however, the NCCB approved the "Pastoral Plan for Pro-life Activities," which was an instruction to bishops to create pro-life committees or citizen lobbies in every Congressional district to lobby against abortion. Responding to a charge of being in conflict of church and state, the bishops issued a statement in 1975 entitled, "Political Responsibility: Reflections on an Election Year," in which they argued that they were not in conflict with the First Amendment but rather were supporting their right to encourage social justice and human rights within the political system.

Regardless of whether it is a moral or a religious issue, logic requires that those who oppose abortion on the grounds that it is the murder of "innocent persons" have a moral imperative to connect this belief with social action. The church believes it is defending the lives of millions of fetuses who have no representation and no power to defend themselves. Given the magnitude of the situation and their official position on abortion, it appears to be a cause the Church is morally compelled to protest.

TACTICS USED TO AFFECT PUBLIC AND PRIVATE ABORTION POLICY

Most political action affecting public and private abortion policy falls under the guise of peaceful demonstrations, political lobbying, litigation, and even letter-writing campaigns. Some of it, however, borders on harassment, disruption, and, occasionally, violence.

One of the most subtle ways in which opponents in the abortion debate try to manipulate their audience is through the use of language.

> I don't know if anyone will agree with me that it's a baby, but I think we're only fooling ourselves when we think people can deal more easily with a "fetus" than with an "unborn child."

Fetus is merely the Latin term for young one in the womb.

We have all kinds of strange terms. When I was in the hospital both times they rarely used the word abortion. They used neat little terms like "termination of the pregnancy" or "removal of the conceptus." They rarely used the word abortion, and they never used the word baby.

Pro-choice words usually avoid the suggestion of a potential person, favoring terms like "contents of the uterus," "fetal matter," or "conceptus," while pro-life words such as "fetus," "unborn baby," or "baby" indicate that what is being aborted is and would have been a human being. Along these same lines, pro-choice uses "pregnant woman" or "woman" instead of "mother."

The word "abortion" deals directly with the issue, in contrast to the pro-choice use of strictly medical language to describe an abortion, such as, "vacuum aspiration," "D & E," or "instillation." These terms deflect the focus away from the possibility that abortion is ending a human life and onto the premise that it is merely terminating an unwanted pregnancy. In contrast, words like "killing," "genocide," "aborticide," and "murder," sometimes used by pro-life members, inflame the issue and keep meaningful debate at a distance.

Right-to-life (anti-abortion) advocates use terms like "baby" rather than "fetus" and often show graphic pictures of the end result of abortion.

Abortion clinics have been the target of individuals and groups opposed to abortion. This women's clinic in Cleveland, Ohio, was destroyed by a fire bomb.

Trying to tag people with pro-life or pro-choice labels further polarizes them, denying them a common ground on which to discuss such a difficult issue. Many viewpoints are not as divergent as the use of such labels implies. For example, "pro-life" suggests that anyone not *pro*-life is *against* life, which is absurd, while *pro*-choice implies that anyone not pro-choice is *against* choice, also absurd. People who are not pro-choice may, in fact, support abortion in one circumstance but not in another. Such labeling is inadequate and fails to consider the whole spectrum of opinion.

Today, almost every major free-standing abortion clinic, especially those in the South and Midwest, is subject to some form of harassment. Pro-life tactics range from the peaceful distribution of antiabortion literature, picketing, and the scheduling of no-show appointments at clinics to disrupt their scheduling of legitimate patients, to physically contacting or blocking patients, and loud demonstrations outside clinics to annoy staff and intimidate patients. Pro-life groups have also been known to stage waiting room sit-ins, jam clinic telephone lines, trace patients and providers in order to subsequently harass them at their homes, vandalize clinic property, and threaten to bomb or set fire to clinic premises, as well as actually doing so.

According to the National Abortion Federation (NAF), between 1977 and 1987, there were over 700 specific acts of violence reported against clinics, amounting to several million dollars worth of damage. In June 1986, for example, an abortion clinic in St. Louis, Missouri, was the victim of arson that caused $100,000 worth of damage to the clinic.[5] Moreover, studies have shown that the rate of complications and recovery time for the women in these clinics substantially increases during periods when the clinic is being harassed.

With no sign of harassment ceasing or even abating, clinics are advised to increase their security and are compelled to pay higher liability insurance premiums. In some cases, they are denied protection and forced to retreat elsewhere. Some local governments, reluctant to tolerate potential violence and harassment, deny licensing to abortion clinics or else make it difficult for them to establish a practice.

One abortion provider, a physician, woke up early one Father's Day to the chanting of "murderer," "abortionist," echoing from his residential street. Outside, riding in open cars, shouting into bullhorns, demonstrators were trying to intimidate him and stop him from performing abortions.

Not all tactics are so intimidating. One of the most common strategies, first developed by Catholics United for Life, is sidewalk counseling, where a self-appointed "counselor" tries to persuade a woman entering an abortion clinic to reconsider her decision by providing her with information about the abortion procedure and fetal development and offering to help her find an alternative. The "counselor" hopes to change the woman's mind about going through with the abortion.

Sidewalk counseling can be effective in changing a woman's mind about abortion. But sometimes, what may have started out as gentle persuasion turns into a last-minute confrontation, seriously harassing abortion patients. Many abortion clinics have to offer escorts to women who are unable to leave their cars without being accosted by a sidewalk counselor handing them a color photograph of a dismembered fetus or screaming at them that they are "murdering their baby."

One of the most effective crusades has been the nationwide establishment of centers that provide counseling and assistance for women not to have an abortion. Centers like Birthright or the Crisis Pregnancy Center program (run by the Christian Action Council, founded by Reverend Billy Graham) encourage women to seek alternatives to abortion, helping them find adoptive homes for their babies, or providing them with financial and emotional support for keeping them.

Unfortunately, a few pro-life groups run deceptive advertising for bogus "clinics" that allege to refer a patient to abortion services, when, in reality, they beseige her with antiabortion literature, films, and so-called "counseling." While some women report being honestly grateful for being persuaded not to have an abortion, many women are in search of a real abortion clinic, and a visit to one of these bogus clinics only adds more stress to the situation. One distraught patient, who was a plaintiff in a suit against a bogus clinic, reported that her "counselor" had shown her slides of severed fetuses, while warning her that the chance of dying from an abortion was high. It was suggested that she pursue other alternatives. Another woman ended up in a hospital with severe physical pain that was attributed to the emotional stress she suffered from her visit to one of these clinics.

With the exception of violence and obvious criminal conduct, many kinds of protest fall within the gray areas of First Amendment protection and are subject to individual court interpretations that vary among jurisdictions. For example, in some areas it is legal for pro-life protesters to enter an abortion clinic waiting room and present leaflets to patients. In other clinics, and especially in hospitals, such political action is considered a disruption to the tranquillity necessary for efficient medical practice and is thus illegal.

In his book, *99 Ways to Stop Abortion,* Joseph Scheidler, a Jesuit priest committed to stopping abortion, warns that violence is wrong and unjustifiable and suggests many other ways to stop abortion. Though violence and illegal harassment are engaged in by only a minority of pro-life activists, the damage they invoke is considerable. What is disturbing is that violent behavior is being increasingly tolerated by more moderate pro-life leaders. Perhaps this is out of frustration that after so many years of abortion, and so many millions of fetuses destroyed, their own peaceful and legal efforts have not stopped abortion.

When legislative reform measures consistently fail, those determined to stop abortion justify their tactics as a moral war above the letter of the law. They frequently compare themselves to the resistance that should have been evident during the Nazi regime in Germany and other dark periods of human history. But such comparisons are not persuasive, since the German public had little recourse against the totalitarian Nazi government. In America, pro-life advocates can continue serving their interests through lobbying, legislation, peaceful demonstrations, and education.

Chapter Eight

WHY WOMEN HAVE ABORTIONS

If the current abortion rate continues, nearly half of all the women in the United States can be expected to have an abortion at least once in their lifetime.[1] Their reasons can be listed and arranged into orderly categories. In general, abortion is either to terminate an unwanted pregnancy, a pregnancy that threatens the health or life of a woman, or a pregnancy that terminates a genetically deformed fetus. The reasons can be divided further by the circumstances: rape, incest, poor timing, economic hardship, single parenthood, and inconvenience, to name a few. But this process of compartmentalizing women's lives, of putting their traumas and conflicts into lists, depersonalizes what they actually experience when they decide to have an abortion.

The following intimate accounts, the likes of which have appeared throughout this book, better illustrate and examine why women feel compelled to have an abortion.

Women have abortions because they are pregnant and single and want to postpone motherhood.

When I was twenty-nine, I had a brief fling with a man whom I had been in love with for years. He was a mime and travelled on the road to make a living. By the time I had discovered my contraceptive method had failed, I was weeks pregnant. At the time, I was unemployed and trying to start out in business as a counselor. I could hardly provide for myself, much less another mouth. I spent a lot of time on my knees praying for guidance as to the right thing to do. . . . My choice to abort the fetus was my only sane alternative. The shame of having an out-of-wedlock child was enormous, especially for my mother.

I could not see carrying a child to term at my age and then giving it up for adoption. My religion says that the child becomes a full fledged person only when it takes the first breath. Until then it does not have "human" standing. I went with what I felt to be spiritually, morally, and economically just.

Five years later, I still feel good about my decision. It kept me from the welfare roles, it kept me sane, it allowed me to work in a way that allows my life to be one of service, not just working to feed a little unwanted and unexpected child.

It is not fair for men to have an hour of pleasure and then leave a woman with twenty years of work. I feel that it is the woman's right to make the choice herself if she can mentally, spiritually, and psychologically be responsible for the raising of her child, and not a matter for governmental legislation.

When I was seventeen, and a senior in high school, I found out that I was pregnant. The boy that I had been seeing was in medical school at the time, and accused me of trying to trap him into marriage. This was absolutely not true; my mother had never discussed anything with me concerning sex, and the word of mouth from other girls was woefully inadequate, for I really knew nothing about contraception.

I went along with an abortion rather than have my parents aware of the shame that their only daughter had brought to them.

I went on to graduate high school, and college, and married, and had children at the proper time in my life, when I could provide a proper home and care for them. By having an abortion, I was able to go on and live a beautiful life. But if that baby had developed and been born, what kind of life would I have ever been able to have?

No person has the right to decide that a young woman [spelled "girl"] should have to carry, bear and care for the result of a foolish liaison with a young man [spelled "boy"]. Why should any young woman have to pay that price for the rest of her life if good and safe medical care could be available?

Women have abortions because they do not feel they can cope with another child at that particular time in their life.

Almost exactly a decade ago, I learned I was pregnant. I was sick in my heart and thought I would kill myself. It was as if I'd been told my body had been invaded by cancer. It seemed that was very wrong. Indeed, for that time and circumstance, my carrying a pregnancy to term and bearing a child into the world would have been very very wrong. I was one and a half years out of a very unhappy marriage (from which I recovered emotionally only after many years, really). I was the mother and sole provider of an eight-year-old boy. It was a struggle for me to be learning that I could actually earn our way in the world. I held several jobs, and was assisted by the Welfare Department from time to time, for medical needs. For only a year I had begun tentatively making new friendships in this town.

I had a safe, legal abortion, paid for by the Welfare Medicaid. Although I wept afterwards for many reasons deep and non-verbal, I have never regretted that

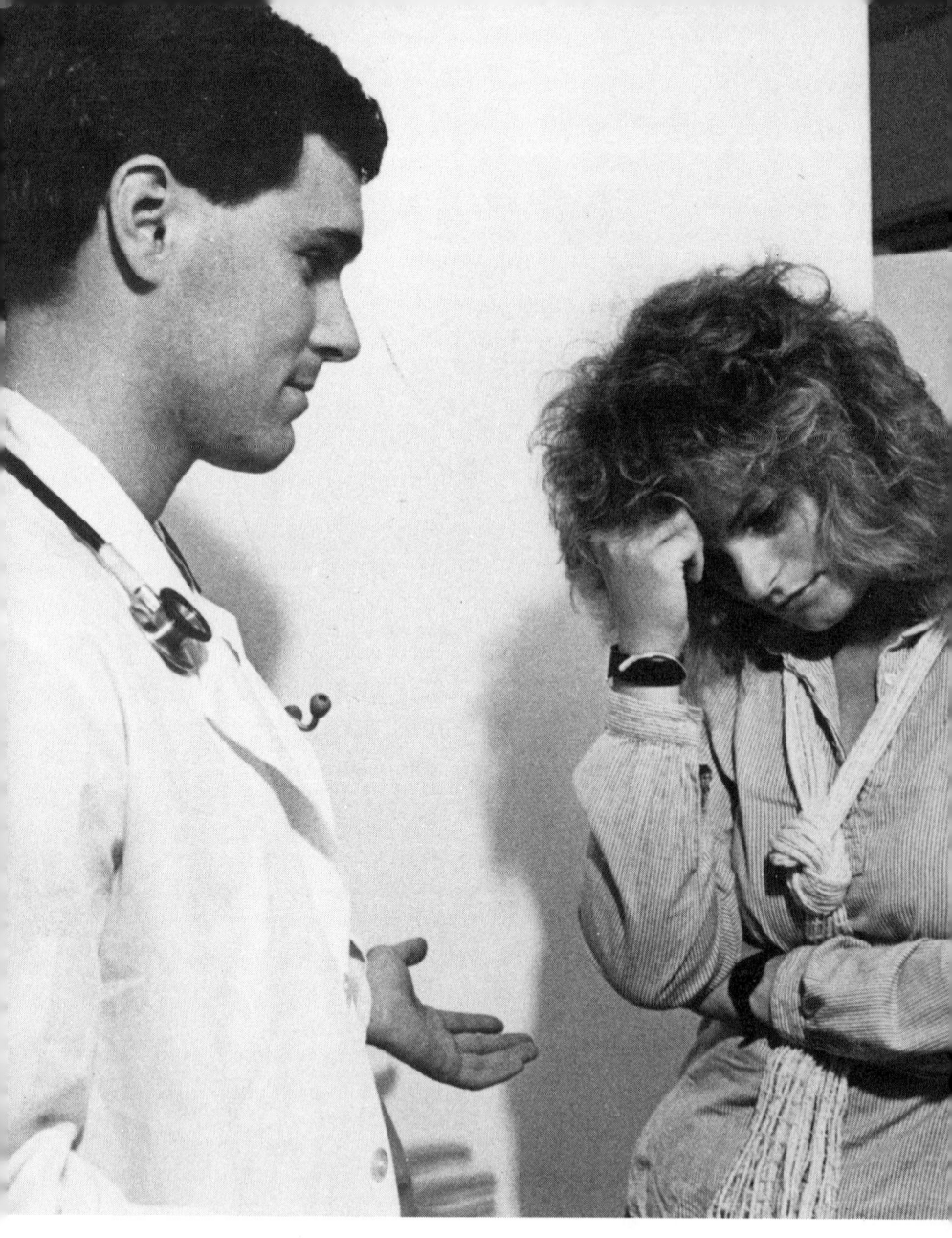

Women confronted with an unwanted pregnancy face a time filled with tremendous anxiety, uncertainty, and ambivalence. Choosing to have an abortion is a painful, difficult decision.

decision. It was right for me at the time. It was one of the first pro-active decisions I had made in behalf of myself, my son, and my real hopes for our future.

It seemed important to tell this story in some bit of detail, to undo the harm caused by superficial categorizing and religious glibness. Life is complex and difficult. In an enlightened society, every woman has the same freedom as every man to manage her life and to create her future.

Women have abortions because they are victims of rape or incest.

I am a twenty-six-year-old single woman. I have had two abortions, one when I was twelve years old, the other when I was thirteen. I got pregnant from my stepfather and my mother's boyfriend. My mother totally denied incest had been happening since I was five.

At the time, I felt having an abortion made my position safer by keeping it hidden. I was a child myself, developing severe emotional problems from living in an intolerable situation from which I knew no escape. I did later escape temporarily by having a nervous breakdown, in which I attempted suicide and was placed in a mental hospital and later a children's home. I could hardly have raised two children, nor would it have been good for them to have taken my place in the home and begin their lives by being repeatedly and brutally raped.

Not having two children has enabled me to leave my home as soon as possible [age seventeen] and go to school to try to improve my life and get off welfare.

In 1971 my sister was pregnant after a very brutal rape. Having been brought up as a conservative Roman Catholic, my family had a very difficult decision to make. The physicians had notified our family that if she went through the full term of her pregnancy, she would not survive it. Abortion was totally against everything that we had been brought up to believe in, so you can imagine how the family felt, and we were all torn at that time.

Our parish priest came over and recommended against abortion, which meant that we had to deal with losing Rose Elizabeth (could that be God's will?).

After much fighting within the family, and endless discussion, the family decided that we couldn't go against the teaching of our church, and my sister's death would be a consequence we would just have to go through.

Today I can't imagine the pyschological trauma Rose Elizabeth must have gone through; she had lost all self-esteem, she was guilt-ridden, and most of the time felt very much alone.

So alone, pregnant, knowing that she would die if she didn't have an abortion, afraid of the embarrassment, the pain, the guilt, she called a close friend who knew of a person who would do the abortion. She decided to wait until we had all left for church, then called her friend to pick her up.

I can still remember opening the door of that old, half-abandoned building, and seeing her laid out on the table, bleeding to death. She never made it out alive.

Women have abortions to preserve their health or their life.

When I was thirty-one, I became pregnant. I had waited a long time for a child, and I wanted it very badly. But something went wrong.

I was sick almost from the beginning. Sometime during the third month, I partially aborted. I was almost into the fifth month when it was deemed necessary to perform a therapeutic abortion.

Because I had been unable to work since the first month, I was forced onto Aid to Families with Dependent Children rolls and Medi-Cal. Had it not been for the Medi-Cal, I would have been unable to afford the abortion.

I would have died had it not been for the abortion. The ability to have an abortion, coupled with the Medi-Cal funding available, saved my life.

Today I am thirty-five. I have a healthy fourteen-month-old daughter.

About 15 percent of women who use birth control will become pregnant. The most reliable methods, like the pill, cause side effects some women cannot or will not tolerate. Sterilization is the most reliable method, but it leaves women with no option to having children in the future. Nor is celibacy a preference for many women.

I was a married woman who was using a diaphragm and a spermicide jelly. My first child was planned, and I was very happy. Slightly more than two years later, I had another planned child. Then I found myself pregnant with a child that would be only seventeen months younger than the second child. I had used my birth control methods assiduously, but to no avail. I accepted the fact of that child and loved it.

Then I got pregnant again. This one would be thirteen months younger than the third child. I was faced with the unpleasant fact that I couldn't stop the babies from coming no matter what I did. I really could not stand the thought of another baby so soon.

I am not a person with a great deal of energy, and this new baby would have strained me to the limit and beyond. Our family doctor gave me an enormous dose of hormone which eventually produced a miscarriage. It was a tremendous relief, and I have never regretted it.

A few women have abortions because if they remain pregnant and bear a child, they might commit suicide.

This is not a letter about an abortion. I wish it were. Instead, it is about an incident which took place over forty years ago in a small mid-western town on the banks of the original "Old Mill Stream."

One night a young girl jumped off the railroad bridge to be drowned in that river. I will always remember the town coming alive with gossip over the fact that she was pregnant and unmarried.

I was enormously moved by what to me was a terrible tragedy. I could imagine the young girl's despair as she made her decision to end her life rather than face the stigma of having an illegitimate birth. You must remember this was a mid-western town where "traditional values"—to use a current phrase—were the only acceptable standards.

I was young and did not even know the term "abortion" at the time. Perhaps the young girl didn't either. Even if she had, there would have been no place in that small town where she could have obtained one.

I still grieve for the girl. She should not have had to pay with her life for that one mistake.

Adoption is an option for some women; so is welfare assistance. But for some women, it is not, and they choose to have an abortion.

When I was only sixteen years old, in 1968, I found myself faced with an unplanned and untimely pregnancy. Abortions were illegal at that time and I did not have the money or resources to know how to go about getting one any other way. When I finally got up the nerve to tell my parents, I was almost four months into the pregnancy. It was at this time that I felt the impending doom of my situation. I was forced to carry the pregnancy to term. During my pregnancy I was treated like a baby machine—an incubator without feelings—who was to produce this child for adoption for another couple who could not have children, for whatever reasons.

I gave birth to a beautiful, healthy baby boy, a child I would never be allowed to touch. My son was placed for adoption within a matter of days after his birth. I am prohibited by law from knowing anything about him or his well-being, but I still think about him and worry about him every day. I don't think very many people understand the sacrifice of having to surrender a child for adoption, knowing records are sealed and you will most likely never see that child again. I don't think any girl or woman (whatever her age) should have to go through the pain, humiliation and heartache of a situation like this.

Six years later I again found myself in an unfortunate position of being pregnant at a time in my life that was all wrong. I made an appointment with Planned Parenthood, and I'll never forget the relief I felt at being able to get a safe, legal abortion. The doctor and nurses couldn't have been more helpful. They made no judgments about my decision and treated me like an intelligent, rational human being. I was only six weeks into the pregnancy when I had the procedure, which was very simple. I've never regretted my decision to have an abortion.

Each year approximately fifteen hundred women have induced abortions because their fetuses were deformed.

Last year I was almost five months pregnant with my first child—a loved, wanted and very well-planned child. Through an ultrasound [test], we discovered the baby had a fetal problem—a cystic hygroma—and that it would not live beyond birth. Fortunately, I was just within the legal deadline for an abortion, so I scheduled one as soon as possible. I had a very painful and long labor, but the hospital staff specialized in late trimester abortions, and they were very competent and sympathetic.

I think about how awful it would have been to find out that the baby was doomed and to have to carry it four more months. Pregnancy takes your whole body, your life; your mind is full of the promise of the future—in this case, only the promise of death.

Ironically, the option to have an abortion gives some women the courage to have children.

In September 1982, after a completely normal pregnancy, I gave birth to a baby girl with spina bifida and severe hydrocephalus. For five days I held my much-wanted and long-awaited daughter in my arms and watched the life drain out of her. My baby was so severely brain-damaged that she was unable to suck, had no awareness of her surroundings and too little brain function to support her life. After five days she died.

The wracking grief and tremendous pain we experienced holding our baby's tiny body seconds after her death and during the months and years since have convinced me that we would never have subjected ourselves to the possibility of a recurrence of this tragedy if I had not had the possibility of a safe, legal abortion available to me.

But since I was able to have prenatal testing tell me that the new fetus I was carrying was healthy, and since otherwise I would have had the option to terminate the pregnancy, I did go ahead with a decision to go through another pregnancy. Sarah was born thirteen months ago and is the delight of my life.

Chapter Nine

THE ETHICAL ISSUE

For these reasons, we decided to choose abortion. This was not a frivolous wasting of potential human life or "abortion on demand" at its worst. It was responsible decision-making. It was moral and conscious living.

The legalization of abortion does not exempt people from behaving morally. It gives them the opportunity to do so. Abortion is a very personal decision—seldom, if ever taken lightly—and one which should be made with responsibility.

It is taking a life. Even though it is not formed, it is the potential, and to me it is still taking a life.

Some people argue that life is a divine blessing which no individual, not even a mother, has the moral right to terminate. Others argue that no individual, not even a fetus, has the right to force a woman to remain pregnant against her will. In the middle are those individuals who believe that what is moral depends on the particular circumstances, such as the viability of the fetus and why the woman wants an abortion.

Only through real debate about abortion ethics can the issue be resolved, or at least understood. Too often each side self-righteously announces its position and closes off any further discussion.

When Carol Gilligan studied the way women determine the morality of abortion, she concluded that most use an ethic of responsibility, a responsibility they feel not only towards their fetus (and its potential future), but towards others as well. They believe that given their particular circumstances at the time of the decision, continuing their pregnancy would seriously hurt others in their life, perhaps their parents, their companions, other children, or themselves.

The only valid excuse for behaving "immorally" is ignorance, not knowing the right way to act, which is different from acting immorally (out of weakness or lack of courage) or being morally uncertain (knowing that it requires knowledge of an ethical principle but being unsure what the principle is). Most women make their decision to have an abortion by exploring their alternatives and ultimately deciding that an abortion is their most moral (or least "immoral") choice. Though they have made the decision by exploring what they consider their alternatives and making what they believe is a moral decision, many women express deep regret over their abortions.

Unfortunately, for some women, their decision to have an abortion is made in such haste or with so little knowledge, that later, when they have had more time to think about the morality of it, they become convinced their abortions were immoral. This leaves them feeling guilty, angry, and remorseful. Proponents of more informed consent suggest that the more information a woman has, the more likely she is to make a moral decision that she can live with not only in the short term but in the future as well.

> Can you imagine how it feels, years later, to see pictures of aborted babies? I thought I would die, seeing what I'd done.

Being a woman who experienced an abortion, I can tell you that withholding information from women that may affect them for the rest of their lives is both dangerous and demeaning. Doctors may explain more about tonsillectomies or appendectomies, than they do about abortions. I really believe that if I had been fully informed, both medically and as to my options, I would have chosen not to abort my baby.

PERSONHOOD

One ethical guideline in our society is that it is immoral—and against the law—to murder another person. Although our society finds certain killings, such as self-defense or "justifiable" wars, morally permissible (there are those who do not agree and find all killing immoral), it does not justify the killing of innocent people. If then, a fetus is considered a person, it is immoral to abort it because that would be the same as killing an innocent person. Furthermore, it is also argued that abortion is immoral because although it might not be killing a person, it is killing a life that has the *potential* to become a person. Still others believe it is immoral to abort a fetus merely because it holds the possibility of being a person.

At what point in its development the fetus becomes a "person" with all the rights that go along with personhood, including the right-to-life, is an important moral question. It is at that point that many people decide that an abortion is immoral.

Scientifically, it is now possible to see that life begins at conception (and ends at death). But is a human life the same as a person? People are taught to respect

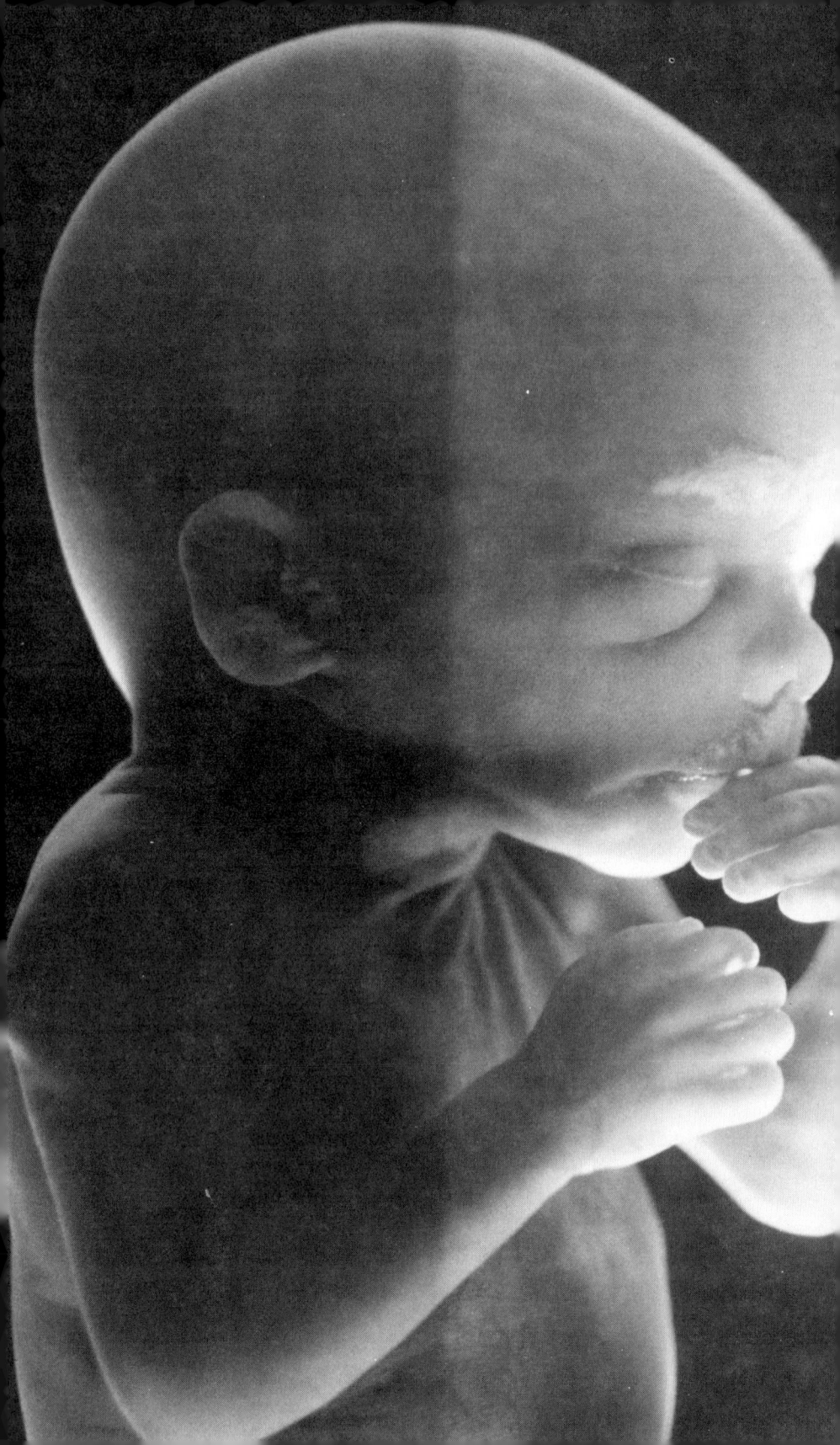

all forms of life, from plants to animals, but that respect is not equal to the rights to which a person is entitled. What value will be placed on life at conception and until viability or birth is at the heart of the question. During the arguments for *Roe* v. *Wade*, the Supreme Court heard such diverse testimony about the value of fetal life that it could not resolve the question of personhood.

> We need not resolve the difficult question of when life begins. When those trained in respective disciplines of medicine, philosophy, and theology are unable to arrive at any consensus, the judiciary, at this point in the development of man's knowledge, is not in a position to speculate as to the answer.
> —The Supreme Court, *Roe* v. *Wade*

Life is a developmental process, from conception to death. But when does personhood begin? At conception? When the heart starts beating? When the fetus can feel pain? When the mother can feel its movements? When it can survive outside the womb? After birth? When it can love? When it can think rationally? There is very little agreement on when personhood begins. Theologians cannot agree; neither can philosophers.

A twelve-week-old fetus. At the heart of the abortion debate is the question of whether a fetus is a "person" with all the rights granted to human beings—particularly the right to life.

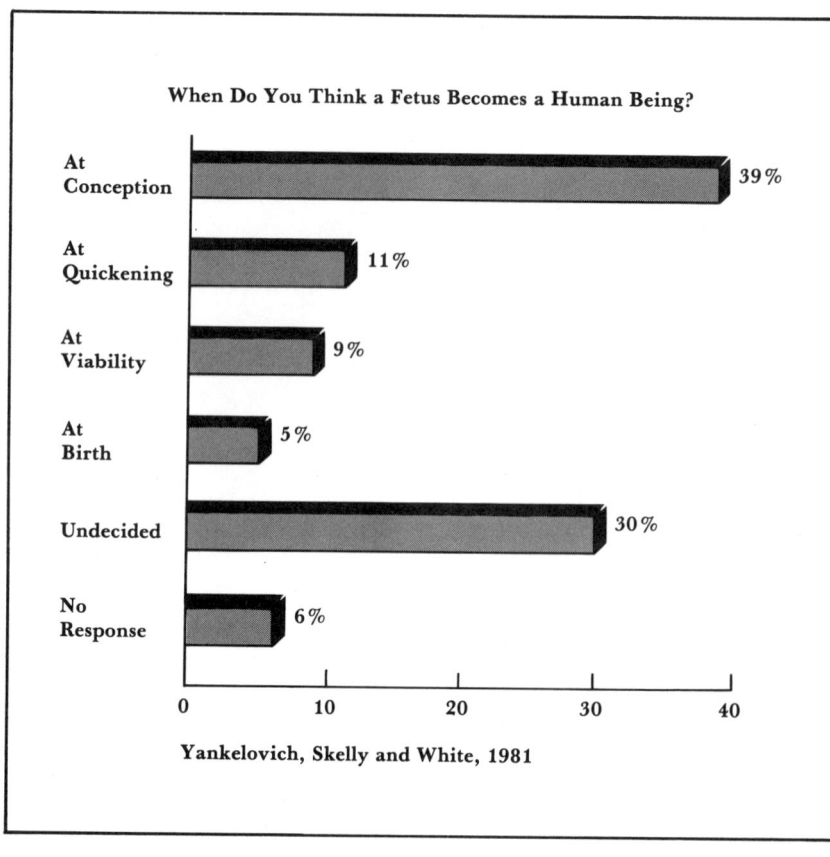

Attributing personhood to the moment of conception makes all abortion immoral. It even renders those forms of birth control that inhibit the fertilized egg's development to be immoral. Moreover, if personhood is not provable, but possible, why take a chance on destroying the life of a fetus that could possibly be a person? And finally, even though the fetus might not be a person, and perhaps is not a person, because it has the potential to be a person can be sufficient reason to protect its right-to-life.

COMPETING MORAL RIGHTS

Even if the fetus is not yet a person, it is still a form of human life, part of the human species, and is valuable from that standpoint alone. Valuable, worthy of respect. But does the respect for that fetus warrant that it should be valued enough to be protected from abortion?

Many ethicists avoid the entire issue of personhood. Regardless of the possibility that the fetus is a person at some stage in its development prior to viability or birth, what is indisputable is that a pregnant woman is a person with moral rights and moral claims. Can she claim moral rights that interfere with the fetus's right-to-life? While the Supreme Court determined a legal way to resolve the issue of competing rights in the law, the moral issue of how to resolve that competition, if there is one, remains.

For many women, pregnancy is a wonderful, fulfilling experience. Even women who do not find it so wonderful are willing to endure it for a child they want and love. But should a woman be expected to put up with pregnancy and the pain of childbirth against her will? No one can be compelled to donate one of his or her organs to save another person's life, so why should a woman be morally compelled to donate the use of her body for nine months, perhaps even risking her health or her life during the period? Surely any woman who endures a pregnancy after being raped and places her baby up for adoption deserves recognition for her selflessness. But as Christine Gudorf suggests, "Each of us must be free to choose our own place and own type of moral heroism."[1]

> It is difficult to adequately describe the difference between a wanted and an unwanted pregnancy. It is something like that difference between darkness and despair, and light and joy.

Pro-life feminist Sidney Callahan disagrees that women are morally entitled to this kind of choice. She writes, "There is a distorted idea of morality when individuals believe they can choose not to be pregnant. Morality also consists of the good and worthy acceptance of the unexpected events life presents. Responsiveness and responsibility to things unchosen are also instances of the highest moral capacity."[2]

Advocates of the fetus's moral right to use its mother's body argue that the fetus is innocent and therefore entitled to be born. It never asked to be born but was conceived by two other people whose rights are not as compelling as the fetus's right to life. After all, those with this view argue, pregnancy is a common occurrence. Though at times inconvenient and even difficult, it seldom costs a woman her life anymore. The majority of abortions are non-therapeutic for the woman yet always cost a fetus its life. On the other hand, failure to acknowledge the impact pregnancy and childbirth can have on a woman trivializes the reasons women seek abortions and ignores the real hardships they often sustain.

What about adoption as an alternative to abortion? If women should not be morally compelled to raise unwanted children, don't they have a moral obligation to place their unwanted children up for adoption? While this argument is persuasive to many, to others it ignores the babies who are difficult to place in adoptive homes as well as the issue of insisting that a woman remain pregnant against her will.

Though most abortions are performed on women who want to terminate their pregnancies, about fifteen hundred abortions are performed annually on women who chose to be pregnant but later decided to terminate the life of their fetus. Through genetic testing, much can be learned about a fetus. Aborting a fetus because it is so disabled it will probably not function beyond a vegetative stage or is destined to a short life filled with pain and suffering may be perceived as a moral act (and may not be). On the other hand, aborting a fetus with Down's Syndrome or "the wrong gender" is perhaps of a different moral order. "Do we wish," Adrienne Asch writes, "to send the message to all such people now living that there should be no more of 'your kind' in the future."[3]

Today, geneticists have found chromosomal markers for Huntington's Chorea, a crippling disease that does not strike until midlife. They have also found markers for alcoholism and colon cancer. At what point is it moral to abort a fetus in order to spare it future suffering? Does a life destined to be lived in blindness, deafness, in a wheelchair, or even drunk morally justify abortion? When a fetus has Down's Syndrome, a genetic disorder that ranges from mild to severe mental disability, who is being spared if it is aborted, the fetus or its parents? Does parenthood come with the right to accept only children who meet certain standards?

Raising a disabled child can be a fulfilling experience and a virtue, but it can also be an enormous strain, one many parents feel is more than they can bear and more than they must morally accept. For disabled children often require much energy and resources, and most of the burden for this falls on their parents, not the community. Each situation is different; many parents, in fact, choose to have babies because they know they have the option of aborting those fetuses that are genetically deformed.

One foundation upon which our liberal political tradition was based comes from John Stuart Mill's moral rule that people have the right to their own bodies, that no one can own another person's body. This idea laid the ground for marriage reform when women were no longer considered to be their husband's property and also for the abolition of slavery. Many of those who support a woman's right to have an abortion base their argument on this same foundation, that a woman must have the right to "bodily integrity," which includes both the right to her body and to the right to control her own reproduction. Unless she has this right, she can never attain equal status with men, for pregnancy and childrearing have a dramatic impact on her life.

> Five years ago I had an abortion. I was thirty years old, childless, and facing a divorce. I became pregnant while using a diaphragm and terminated the pregnancy five to six weeks after conception. I decided to have an abortion rather than carry the pregnancy to term because I was not financially, emotionally, nor physically able to raise a child by myself.
> At the time, I did not want to have a child. In addition, I did not have the social support to help me through the overwhelming stress and isolation of poverty, single parenthood, and loss of my career. I worked in a biochemistry laboratory with chemicals which cause cancer and birth defects. I would have had to quit my job and seek employment less hazardous to a developing fetus or to a nursing baby. Women still receive only about sixty percent of the salary of a man, and a pregnant woman is an even less desirable employee.

One belief is that it is a moral right and a moral duty for women to bear children because it is natural for them to do so; "biological destiny," this imperative is so often called. Is forcing motherhood on women who don't choose it or on women who find it an incredible hardship immoral? For many women, untimely motherhood makes it difficult for them to continue their education, to secure a job or to pursue a career. For many women, in fact, motherhood ensures their place in poverty, as the increasing "feminization of poverty" suggests. To many people, this potential to become mothers is not a morally compelling reason to assume the role. Abortion allows women to control when and if they will be mothers and to visualize a world where they are autonomous and in as much control of their own destiny as possible. Yet such control is perceived as immoral for all those people who believe that motherhood remains part of natural law.

PRIVATE VERSUS PUBLIC MORALITY

A key debate in the abortion issue is exactly who shall be a "moral agent," the party who decides whether or not an abortion is right or wrong. Some people believe it should be reserved only for those affected by the decision. Both a woman and her fetus are affected by an abortion, yet the fetus is unable to defend its right to life. Like others who are incapable of making rational decisions—the comatose, the senile, the severely mentally disabled—a fetus is vulnerable and dependent on others to make its moral decisions. Ethicist Beverly Harrison asserts that unless and until a woman is her own moral agent in abortion decisions, "she can never have equal status." On the other hand, if a fetus and others in society who are among the meek have no protection, have lives that are not valued equally with the lives of those who are able to defend themselves, then it is possible for all life to be devalued.

The Supreme Court claims that abortion is a private issue, out of the realm of the state. It has upheld a woman's right to have an abortion without consulting her spouse and has ensured her alternatives to consulting her parents. But is abortion a private moral matter? Surely, pregnancy affects a woman more than any other individual. In our society, it is women who assume the greater portion of childrearing, from the time of infancy until adulthood. Yet, although a woman bears the greatest responsibility for children, she is not alone. Men are expected to help, at least financially; the public is expected to educate and perhaps house, feed, and provide medical assistance for children. Yet none of these other parties have the legal right to interfere with a woman's decision to have an abortion. But do any of these responsibilities they are expected to assume give them any moral rights?

RIGHT TO RELIGIOUS FREEDOM

Religion is the source of many of our ethical principles. Yet the major religions have such diverse beliefs on abortion, even within their own organizations, that the law cannot possibly reflect one group without morally offending another. What is at issue is not just whether abortion is moral or immoral, but also whether it is universally moral or immoral. Many religious groups support the morality of abortion, so what is at issue, therefore, is not its morality, but whether any religious group has the right to impose its morality about abortion on another group.

If a group, such as the Catholic Church, believes there is a universal truth, a natural law, that applies to everyone, regardless of the individual's particular conviction, then it is understandable how they would be unwilling to tolerate abortion at all.

The First Amendment guarantees that no group may impose its beliefs on another group or individual. Many different religious denominations flourish under our pluralistic tradition; it is part of America's strength. A crucial issue in the abortion debate then is whether or not abortion is actually a moral issue or whether it is limited to religious and philosophical examination. Thirty-three religious groups belong to the Religious Coalition for Abortion Rights because they share a belief that abortion, at least under certain circumstances, is moral.

> In our Baptist tradition, the integrity of each person's conscience must be protected. Therefore, we believe that abortion must be a matter of responsible, personal decision.
> —American Baptist Churches, U.S.A.

> On religious, moral, and humanitarian grounds, therefore, we arrived at the view that it is far better to end an unwanted pregnancy than to encourage the evils resulting from forced pregnancy and childbearing.
> —American Friends Service Committee

> The fundamental right to privacy applies to contraception, to avoid unintended pregnancy as well as to freedom of choice on abortion to prevent an unwanted birth.
> —American Jewish Congress

> Any decision for an abortion should be made as early as possible, generally within the first trimester of pregnancy, for reasons of the woman's health and safety. Abortions later in pregnancy are an option, particularly in the case of women of menopausal age who do not discover they are pregnant until the second trimester, women who discover through fetal diagnosis that they are carrying a fetus with a grave genetic disorder, or women who did not seek or have

access to medical care during the first trimester. At the point of fetal viability, the responsibilities set before us in regard to the fetus begin to shift. Prior to viability, human responsibility is stewardship of life-in-development under the guidance of the Holy Spirit. Once the fetus is viable, its potential for physically autonomous human life means that the principle of inviolability can be applied.
—Presbyterian Church, U.S.A.

When an unacceptable pregnancy occurs, a family, and most of all the pregnant woman, is confronted with the need to make a difficult decision. We believe that continuance of a pregnancy which endangers the life or health of the mother, or poses other serious problems concerning the life, health, or mental capability of the child to be, is not a moral necessity. In such case, we believe the path of mature Christian judgment may indicate the advisability of abortion.
—United Methodist Church

SOUND REASONING

Sound reasoning is required if the abortion issue is to be honestly debated, as indeed it must be. Many ethicists have cited excellent reasons why abortions may be immoral, and this chapter has only been able to touch on a very few, basic debates. There are a few arguments that do get mentioned by either side that are not always logical, or if they are logical, they are inappropriate. The following is a sample of some of these commonly used arguments.

The first type is called a *slippery slope argument*. This implies that when a first step is taken down a "slippery slope," the rest of the steps will be quickly descended also. Although such arguments are indeed logical, there is no evidence that they are inevitable. In fact, what the argument ignores is how many measured steps are taken not to go down the slippery slope. A simple example of the slippery slope is that if you kill a fly, you will "slip down the slope" and inevitably kill your pet canary. A more complicated version is that there are enough nuclear weapons to annihilate the world; therefore, it will happen. It is logical that it can happen, and it is feared that it will, but it is not necessarily *true* that it will.

The typical slippery slope argument used in abortion debate is that legal abortion is the first step down the slope towards killing off socially useless people like the comatose, the terminally ill, even the poor or racially "inferior." That is, at heart, a serious argument, because the real concern is that allowing abortion might decrease a society's concern for all life and be reflected in its attitudes towards infanticide, mercy killing, or genocide.

While abortion has led to more abortion, there is no evidence that it will lead down the slope to mercy killing, genocide, or infanticide, all of which remain illegal. During the same years that abortion was legalized, many states abolished capital punishment.

Another argument frequently heard in the abortion debate is the case of Beethoven's mother. Here was a woman, suffering from tuberculosis, married to a man with syphilis, and living in abject poverty. She has already given birth to four children, one blind, one deaf and mute, and one suffering from tuberculosis. Two of these children have died. Pregnant with the fifth, should she have had an abortion? If Mrs. Beethoven had had an abortion, she would have aborted what was to become Ludwig van Beethoven, one of the world's musical geniuses. Beethoven suffered from Paget's disease, a genetic disorder that caused him to go deaf. If Mrs. Beethoven had been alive today and able to undergo genetic counseling and diagnose this disease, might she have had an abortion for that reason?

Perhaps if Mrs. Beethoven had access to a safe, legal abortion, she might still have elected to give birth. This argument, and the equally deplorable argument given by the pro-choice who counter that perhaps Adolf Hitler's mother should have had an abortion, totally ignores the slim chance that any woman's fetus will grow up to be either a genius or a lunatic. Many women who have had abortions mourn the lost opportunities to know an individual who will never be. Other women who have decided against abortions have raised children they deeply loved. There are enough compelling arguments for either side to use without resorting to blatantly outrageous ones.

One of the most effective arguments used against the right to abortion is the analogy to the Nazi Holocaust. This argument is objectionable not because it is necessarily illogical (though portions of it are), but rather because it is particularly offensive to those who have survived the Holocaust and to the memory of those who did not. Many scholars believe that the Holocaust stands alone in history.

Abortion is a moral issue that questions the intrinsic value and meaning of life itself. In so doing, it is an important, though complex, social and moral issue. It has an enormous impact on millions of people, not only in the public and political arena, but certainly, as the personal testimonies throughout the book illustrate, in private lives as well.

How one individual perceives the issue, how one individual feels about the morality or immorality of abortion, how one individual respects the right to choice or is outraged by the fetuses aborted since *Roe* v. *Wade* may seem to matter little, except to that one individual.

But it matters a great deal, because in a democracy, the structure of a society, the unseen forces that shape its laws and the tangible services it makes available to its citizens, are a reflection of the sum of all of its individuals. A society can be no stronger than its weakest link, no more powerful than the least vulnerable, no more moral than the immorality it tolerates. Those who are not part of the solution are part of the problem. The abortion debate cannot be ignored, for ignorance can never be moral. It must be debated honestly, intelligently, and continuously.

SOURCE NOTES

Chapter One
1. Although Norma McCorvey originally claimed that she had been raped by three men and a woman, she never filed charges, nor did her lawyers use the rape as a defense in her case. In 1987, in an interview with a newspaper columnist, Norma McCorvey retracted her story and supposedly revealed the truth about her story. Noble, "Plaintiff in key abortion case now denies she was a rape victim," *New York Times*, 9 September 1987. See also "Would *Roe* Go?" *Time*, 21 September 1987:14–15.
2. Most of what we know about common-law right of abortion derives from the pioneering work done by Professor Cyril Means of New York University Law School.
3. Luker, *Abortion and the Politics of Motherhood*, 80–81.

Chapter Two
1. *Roe* v. *Wade*, p. 177.
2. Rubin, *Abortion, Politics, and the Courts*, 126.
3. "Judge Refuses to Allow Abortion for Eleven-Year-Old," *Daily Advocate*, 24 October 1981.

Chapter Three
1. The two quotations are from interviews in Franke's *The Ambivalence of Abortion*.
2. *New Republic*, 27 January 1986.
3. Francke. *The Ambivalence of Abortion*, 56.
4. Ibid., 65.

5. This quotation is an excerpt from a letter written by a woman who had an abortion. Similar excerpts appear throughout the book. Unless otherwise noted, these are original letters that are on public record and have been received by both the National Abortion Rights Action League (as part of their "Abortion Rights: Silent No More" campaign) and Senator Gordon Humphrey (R-NH). Senator Humphrey's letters are part of a campaign to pass an informed consent bill in Congress, and they appear in the *Congressional Record*. The letters in this book are from May 14, 1985, to November 11, 1986 (the majority are from September and October, 1986).
6. National Abortion Federation (NAF), *What Is Abortion Fact Sheet*.

Chapter Four
1. Henshaw, Forrest, and Van Vort, "Abortion Services in the U.S. 1984–85," *Fam. Planning*, 19(2):64.
2. Ibid.
3. NAF, *Economics of Abortion Fact Sheet*.
4. Nestor and Gold, "Public Funding," *Fam. Planning*, 16(3):133.
5. "Rewriting the Social Contract," *New York Times*, 12 April 1987.
6. Nestor and Gold, op. cit.
7. "Contraception and Abortion Costs," *Fam. Planning*, 18(1):37.

Chapter Five
1. Henshaw," "Induced Abortion," *Fam. Planning*, 18(6):250.
2. Tietze and Henshaw, *Induced Abortion: A World Review*.
3. Forrest, "Unintended Pregnancy," *Fam. Planning*, 19(2):76.
4. "More Than 50 Percent of Pregnancies in U.S. Unintended," *Ob. Gyn. News*, 19(1):40.
5. Adamek, *Incidence of Induced Abortions*.
6. Forrest, 76.
7. Westoff et al., "Abortions Preventable by Contraceptive Practice," *Fam. Planning*, 13(5):221.
8. Ibid.
9. Center for Disease Control, *Abortion Surveillance*, 1981, 46.
10. Henshaw, "Characteristics, 1982–83," *Fam. Planning Perspectives*, 19(1):6.
11. Henshaw, "Characteristics of U.S. Women Having Abortions, 1982–1983," *Fam. Planning*, 19(1):5–9.
12. Ibid.
13. Tietze and Henshaw, *Induced Abortion*, 73.

Chapter Six
1. "Little or No Changes in Attitudes on Abortion." *Fam. Planning*, 17(2):6.

2. Adamek, "Public Opinion," unpublished paper, Kansas State University.
3. National Abortion Rights Action League (NARAL), *Legal Abortion:* 63.
4. Adamek, *Abortion and Public Opinion*, 12.
5. Petchevsky, *Abortion and Women's Choice*, 90.

Chapter Seven
1. Hurst, *History of Abortion in the Catholic Church*, 11.
2. Ibid., 15.
3. Ibid.
4. Ibid., 19.
5. Kort, Terrorism, *Ms*, May 1987:49.

Chapter Eight
1. Forrest, op. cit., 77.

Chapter Nine
1. Gudorf, "Making Distinctions," *Christianity and Crisis*, 14 July 1986:243.
2. Callahan and Callahan, eds., *Understanding Differences*, 107.
3. Asch, "Real Moral Dilemmas," Ibid., 237.

BIBLIOGRAPHY

Abortion. 1985. *Newsweek.* (14 January):26.

Abortion clinics' toughest cases. 1987. *Medical World News.* (9 March):55–61.

Abortion fatalities could be prevented by earlier diagnosis of hemorrhage. 1984. *Family Planning Perspectives.* 19(6):283–84.

Abortions as currently performed do not appear to increase the risk of subsequent miscarriage. 1986. *Family Planning Perspectives.* 18(5):231–32.

Abortions today. 1985. *American Medical News.* (1 Feb.):271.

Adamek, Raymond J. 1986. *Abortion and public opinion in the United States.* Washington, D.C.: National Right to Life Educational Trust Fund.

———. 1984. Incidence of induced abortion in the U.S. prior to and after the Supreme Court decision. Unpublished paper (3 Oct.).

Akron Pregnancy Distress Center Newsletter, April 1987.

American adults' approval of legal abortion has remained virtually unchanged since 1972. 1985. *Family Planning Perspectives.* 17(4):181.

American Civil Liberties Union (ACLU). 1986. *Parental Notice Laws.* New York: Reproduction Freedom Project, ACLU.

———. 1986. *Preserving the right to choose: How to cope with violence and disruption at abortion clinics.* New York: Reproduction Freedom Project, ACLU.

———. *The so-called human life amendment*. New York: Reproductive Freedom Project, ACLU.

Andrusko, Dave. 1983. *To rescue the future*. New York: Life Cycle Books.

Andrusko, Dave, ed. 1985. *Call to conscience*. Washington, D.C.: The National Right to Life Committee.

Annas, George J. 1986. Pregnant women as fetal containers. Hastings Center Report. (December):13–14.

Beal v. Doe. (1977). 432 U.S. 438

Beauchamp, Tom L., and James F. Childress. 1983. *Principles of biomedical ethics*. New York: Oxford Univ. Press.

Bergel, Gary. 1986. *When you were formed in secret*. Reston, Virginia: Intercessors for America.

Berger, Charlene, Dolores Gold, David Andres, Peter Gillett, and Robert Kinch. 1984. Abortion. *Family Planning Perspectives*. 16(2):70–74.

Boston Women's Health Book Collective. 1984. *Our bodies, ourselves*. New York: Simon & Schuster.

Brandsen, Cheryl Kreykes. 1985. *A case for adoption*. Grand Rapids, Michigan: Betheny Christian Services.

Brozan, Nadine. 1984. Study of abortion frequency. *The New York Times*. (6 May).

Callahan, Daniel. 1970. *Abortion: Laws, choice & morality*. New York: Macmillan.

Callahan, Daniel, and Sidney Callahan, eds. 1984. *Understanding differences*. New York: Plenum Press.

Callahan, Sidney. 1987. A Pro-life feminist makes her case. *Utne Reader*. (March–April):104–08.

Catholics United for Life. *The best way to save babies*. New Hope, Kentucky: Catholics United for Life.

Cheryenak, Frank A., et al. 1984. When is termination of pregnancy during the third trimester morally justifiable? *New England Journal of Medicine*. 310(8):501–4.

Congressional Quarterly (CQ). 1986. *Congressional Quarterly's guide to the U.S. Constitution*. Washington, D.C.: CQ.

———. 1986. *This Constitution*. Washington, D.C.: CQ.

Connery, John. 1977. *Abortion: The development of the Roman Catholic perspective*. New Orleans: Loyola Univ. Press.

Contraception and abortion costs are tiny portion of U.S. health spending. 1986. *Family Planning Perspectives*. 18(1):37–38.

Couple to Couple League. 1986. *Legacy of Margaret Sanger*. Cincinnati, Oh.: Couple to Couple League.

Devereux, George. 1955. *A study of abortion in primitive societies*. New York: Julian Press.

Diamant, Anita. 1982. Moral abortion. *Boston Phoenix*. (16 Feb.)

Dissenting opinions. 1986. *New York Times*. (12 June).

Doe v. Bolton. (1973). 410 U.S. 179

Dolnick, Edward. 1985. Tests that reveal fetal defects are raising ethical questions. *Boston Globe*. (29 April):37.

Donovan, Patricia. 1985. The holy war. *Family Planning Perspectives*. 17(1):5–9.

———. 1983. Judging teenagers: How minors fare when they seek court-authorized abortions. *Family Planning Perspectives*. 15(6):258–67.

———. 1984. Wrongful birth and wrongful conception. *Family Planning Perspective*. 16(2):64–69.

Don't squeal on me! 1984. *The Watch*. Waltham, Mass.: Brandeis Univ. (20 March):12–13.

Durshlag, Melvin, and William Marshall. 1987. The U.S. Constitution. Lecture. Peninsula, Oh. (23 Janu.)

Ehrenreich, Barbara. 1985. Hers: Is abortion really a 'moral dilemma'?. *New York Times*. (7 Feb.)

Encouraging birth control may reduce number of abortions 50 percent. 1982. *Ob/Gyn News*. (15 March).

English, Deirdre. 1981. The war against choice, *Mother Jones Reprint Service*. (Feb.–March).

Falik, Marilyn. 1983. *Ideology and abortion policy politics*. New York: Praeger.

Forrest, J.D., and S.K. Henshaw. 1987. The harassment of U.S. abortion providers. *Family Planning Perspectives*. 19(1):9–12.

Francke, Linda Bird. 1978. *The ambivalence of abortion*. New York: Random House.

Francome, Colin. 1984. *Abortion freedom*. London: George Allen Univ.

Freedman, Samual G. 1987. Suspect in New York abortion-clinic bombings. *New York Times*. (7 May):18.

Fuchs, Victor R., and Leslie Perreault. 1986. Expenditures for reproduction-related health care. *JAMA*. 255(1):76–79.

George, Richard A. 1986. Post-abortion depression. *Right to Life Educational Foundation*. 4(Fall):8.

Gilligan, Carol. *In a different voice*. Boston: Harvard University Press, 1982.

Gould, Carol C., and Marx W. Wartofsky, eds. 1976. *Women and philosophy*. New York: G.P. Putnam's Sons.

Grimes, David A. 1984. Second-trimester abortions in the U.S. *Family Planning Perspectives*. 16(6):260–5.

Grisez, Germain, and Joseph Boyle. 1979. *Life and death with liberty and justice*. Notre Dame, Ind.: Notre Dame Univ.

Harmon and Weiss. 1986. *The threat to Roe: A legal analysis*. Washington, D.C.: National Abortion Rights Action League.

Harris v. McRae. (1980). 100 S.Cr. 2671

Harrison, Barbara Grizzuti. 1980. Hers. *New York Times* (5 May).

Harrison, Beverly Wildung. 1983. *Our right to choose: Toward a new ethic of abortion*. Boston: Beacon Press.

Henshaw, Stanley K. 1987. Characteristics of U.S. women having abortions, 1982–1983. *Family Planning Perspectives*. 19(1):5–9.

———. 1982. Freestanding abortion clinics. *Family Planning Perspectives*. 14(5):248–56.

———. 1986. Induced abortion: A worldwide perspective. *Family Planning Perspectives*. 18(6):250–54.

———. 1986. Trends in abortions, 1982–84. *Family Planning Perspectives*. 18:34.

Henshaw, Stanley K., Nancy J. Binkin, Ellen Blaine, and Jack C. Smith. 1985. A portrait of American women who obtain abortions. *Family Planning Perspectives*. 17(2):90–95.

Henshaw, Stanley K., Jacqueline Darroch Forrest, and Jennifer Van Vort. 1982. Abortion services in the U.S., 1979–80. *Family Planning Perspectives.* 14(1):4–15.

Henshaw, Stanley K., and Lynn S. Wallish. 1984. Medicaid cutoff and abortion services for the poor. *Family Planning Perspectives.* 16(4):170–80.

Hogue, Carol J. Rowland, Willard Cates, Jr., and Christopher Tietze. 1983. Impact of vacuum aspiration abortion on future childbearing. *Family Planning Perspectives.* 15(3):119–25.

Hurst, Jane. 1987. *History of abortion in the Catholic Church.* Washington, D.C.: Catholics for Free Choice.

Imber, Jonathan B. 1986. *Abortion and the private practice of medicine.* New Haven: Yale Univ. Press.

Inherited Alzheimer's disease is linked to chromosome defect. 1987. *Cleveland Plain Dealer.* (20 Feb.):17.

Jones, Elise F., ed. 1986. *Teenage pregnancy in industrialized countries.* New Haven: Yale Univ. Press.

Kasaian, John J. 1979. *Pocket dictionary of legal words.* New York: Doubleday.

Kohn, Richard. 1981. *The church in a democracy: Who governs?* Washington, D.C.: Catholics for Free Choice.

Kort, Michael. 1987. Terrorism on the front line at an abortion clinic. *Ms.* (May).

Lake, Randall A. 1986. The metaethical framework of anti-abortion rhetoric. *Signs.* (Spring):478–99.

Landy, Uta, and Sarah Lewit. 1982. Administrative, counseling and medical practices in national abortion federation facilities. *Family Planning Perspectives* 14(5):257–62.

League of Women Voters. 1982. *Public policy on reproductive choices.* Washington D.C.: League of Women Voters Education Fund.

Leary, Warren E. 1984. Abortion has no effect on fertility. *Boston Sunday Globe.* (12 February):17.

Linden, Karin. 1983. *Moscow women.* New York: Pantheon.

List of clinics hit since 1982. 1985. *Boston Sunday Globe.* (6 Jan.).

Luker, Kristin. 1984. *Abortion and the politics of motherhood.* Univ. of Calif. Press.

———. 1975. *Taking chances: Abortion and the decision not to contracept.* Univ. of Calif. Press.

Lutherans for Life. *Silent Abortions.* Libertyville, Ill.: Lutherans for Life.

Maher v. Roe. (1977). 432 U.S. 464

The making and faking of "The silent scream" 1985. *Off Our Backs.* (April):11.

McDonnell, Kathleen. 1984. *Not an easy choice.* Boston: South End Press.

———. 1987. Pro-choice feminists must open up the abortion debate. *Utne Reader.* (March–April):109–14.

McLean, Gary N., ed. 1983. *Comprehensive theological perspectives on abortion.* Minneapolis: Planned Parenthood of Minneapolis.

Melton, Gary B., ed. 1986. *Adolescent Abortion: Psychological and Legal Issues.* Univ. of Nebraska Press.

Miller, Elizabeth. 1985. *Religious liberty and abortion.* Washington, D.C.: Religious Coalition for Abortion Rights Educational Fund.

Mohr, James C. 1978. *Origins and evolution of national policy 1800–1900.* New York: Oxford Univ. Press.

More than 50 percent of pregnancies in U.S. unintended. 1984. *Ob/Gyn News.* 19(1):40.

Most Americans remain opposed to abortion ban and continue to support women's right to decide. 1984. *Family Planning Perspectives.* 16(5):233–34.

Muller, Charlotte F. 1978. Insurance coverage of abortion, contraception and sterilization. *Family Planning Perspectives.* 10:(4):71–77.

Murphy, Jamie. 1987. Tracing fragile X Syndrome. *Time.* (16 March):78.

Nathanson, Bernard N. 1979. *Aborting america.* New York: Pinnacle.

National Abortion Federation (NAF). 1986. *Fact Sheets.* Washington, D.C.: NAF.

———. 1987. *Fourteen years of legal abortion.* Washington, D.C.: NAF.

———. 1986. *Keeping abortion services legal, accessible and safe.* Washington, D.C.: NAF.

———. 1986. *Safety of abortion fact sheet.* Washington, D.C.: NAF.

———. *Standards of abortion care.* Washington, D.C.: NAF.

———. 1986. *What is abortion fact sheet.* Washington, D.C.: NAF.

National Abortion Rights Action League (NARAL). *Constitutional aspects of the right to limit childbearing.* Washington, D.C.: NARAL.

National Organization for Women. 1983. An abbreviated chronology of reproductive rights 2600 B.C.–present. *Boston NOW Newsletter.* (July–Aug.–Dec.).

National Right to Life. 1986. *National right to life handbook.* Denver: National Right to Life Conventions.

———. 1985. *The silent scream: Documenting abortion from the victim's perspective.* Washington, D.C.: National Right to Life Education Trust Fund.

Nestor, Barry, and Rachel Benson Gold. 1984. Public funding of contraceptive, sterilization and abortion services. *Family Planning Perspectives.* 16(3):128–33.

No increased risk of spontaneous abortion found among women with a previous induced abortion. 1981. *Family Planning Perspectives.* 13(5):238.

Noble, Kenneth B. 1987. Plaintiff in key abortion case now denies she was a rape victim. *New York Times* (9 September).

Noonan, John T., Jr. 1979. *Abortion in America.* Toronto: Life Cycle Books.

Paige, Connie. 1983. *The Right to Lifers.* New York: Summit.

Paltrow, Lynn M. 1984. A review of advances in reproductive and neonatal technology as they relate to abortion rights, unpublished paper. Washington, D.C.: National Abortion Rights Action League.

Pellauer, Mary, Beverly Wildung Harrison, Adrienne Asch, Elinor Lockwood Yeo, Christine Gudorf, Byllye Avery, and Rosalind Pollack Petchevsky. 1986. Thinking about abortion: A C & C forum. *Christianity and Crisis.* (14 July):227–50.

Petchevsky, Rosalind Pollack. 1985. *Abortion and women's choice.* Boston: Northeastern Univ. Press.

Planned Parenthood of Massachusetts. *Medicaid funding of abortion.* Massachusetts: Planned Parenthood.

Poelker v. Doe. (1977). 432 U.S. 519

Pollitt, Katha. 1987. Men and abortion. *Utne Reader.* (March–April):116–17.

Rabbis share views on abortion. 1985. *Jewish Reporter.* (March)

Reagan, Ronald. 1984. *Abortion and the conscience of the nation.* New York: Thomas Nelson Publishers.

Religious Coalition for Abortion Rights. 1978. *How we stand.* Washington, D.C.

———. *The Hyde amendment.* Washington, D.C.: Religious Coalition for Abortion Rights Educational Fund.

———. 1983. *Religious freedom and the abortion controversy.* Washington D.C.: Religious Coalition for Abortion Rights.

Rhoden, Nancy K., 1985. Late abortion and technological advances in fetal viability. *Family Planning Perspectives.* 17(4):160–64.

Risk of ectopic pregnancy high after abortions, PID or both. 1982. *Ob/Gyn News* (14 July).

Roe v. Wade. (1973). 410 U.S. 113

Rooks, Judith P. 1984. The other Supreme Court case: *Doe v. Bolton. Womenwise.* (Fall).

Rothman, Barbara Katz. 1987. The abortion problem as doctors see it. *Hastings Center Report.* (Feb.):36.

———. 1982. How science is redefining parenthood. *Ms.* (July–August):154–58.

———. 1986. *The tentative pregnancy.* New York: Viking Penguin.

Rothstein, Polly, and Marian Williams. 1983. *Choice: Legal abortion.* Washington, D.C.: National Abortion Rights Action League.

Rubin, Eva R. 1982. *Abortion, politics, and the courts.* Westport, Conn.: Greenwood Press.

Scheidler, Joseph. 1985. *Ninety-nine ways to stop abortion.* Lake Bluff, Ill.: Regnery Books.

Schmeck, Harold M. 1987. Geneticists put their fingers on disease factors. *Cleveland Plain Dealer.* (19 April):7.

Shattuck, John H.F. 1977. *Rights of privacy.* Skokie, Ill.: National Textbook Co.

Shostak, Arthur B. and Gary McLouth. 1984. *Men & Abortion.* NY: Praeger.

Simmons, Paul D. 1986. *A theological response to fundamentalism on the abortion issue.* Washington, D.C.: Religious Coalition for Abortion Rights Educational Fund.

Swomley, John. 1985. *Six ethical questions.* Washington, D.C.: Religious Coalition for Abortion Rights Education Fund.

———. 1986. *Theology and politics.* Washington, D.C.: Religious Coalition for Abortion Rights Educational Fund.

Subsidized abortions save taxpayers money. 1986. *Womenwise.* (Summer).

Tatalovich, Raymond, and Byron W. Daynes. 1981. *The politics of abortion.* New York: Praeger.

A technical knockout for parental notification. 1987. *Family Planning Perspectives.* 19(1):36–37.

Thompson, Judith Jarvis. 1971. A defense of abortion. *Philosophy and Public Affairs.* 44–66.

Tietze, Christopher. 1984. Public health effects of legal abortions on the U.S. *Family Planning Perspectives.* 16(1).

Tietze, Christopher, and Stanley K. Henshaw. 1986. *Induced abortion: A world review.* New York: Alan Guttmacher Institute.

U.S. Center for Disease Control, Dept. of Health and Human Services. 1986. *Abortion statistics, U.S. 1982–83.* Atlanta, Ga.: GPO.

———. 1986. *Abortion statistics, U.S. 1982–83. Supplement.* Atlanta, Ga.: GPO.

———. 1985. *Abortion surveillance.* Atlanta, Ga.: GPO (November).

———. 1986. *Abortion surveillance: Preliminary analysis—U.S. 1982–83.* (August) 35(288):788–988.

U.S. National Research Council of the National Academy of Sciences. 1986. *Risking the future: Adolescent sexuality, pregnancy and childbearing.* Washington, D.C.: GPO.

Wallis, Claudia. 1987. Is mental illness inherited? *Time.* (8 March):67.

Weisman, Carol S., Constance A. Nathanson, Martha Ann Teitelbaum, Gary A. Chase, and Theodore M. King. 1986. Abortion attitudes and performance among male and female obstetrician-gynecologists. *Family Planning Perspectives* 18(2):67–73.

Wertham, Fredric. 1980. *The German euthanasia program.* Cincinnati: Hayes Publishing.

Westoff, Christopher F., Jane S. DeLung, Noreen Goldman, and Jacqueline Darroch Forrest. 1981. Abortions preventable by contraceptive practice. *Family Planning Perspectives.* 13(5):220–23.

When counseling becomes harassment. 1987. *NAF Update.* (Winter):4.

Whose right to choose? 1987. *Insight.* (26 Jan.):16–17.

Wilkie, J.C., Dr. and Mrs. 1985. *The handbook of abortion.* Cincinnati: Hayes Publishing.

Willis, Ellen. 1983. The politics of abortion. *In These Times.* (15 June).

———. 1985. Putting women back into the abortion debate. *Resist Newsletter.* (September):3–6.

Wogaman, J. Philip. 1977. Abortion as a theological issue. *Washington Post.* (16 August).

Wohl, Lisa Cronin. 1984. Antiabortion violence on the rise. *Ms.* (October):135–40.

Women exposed to AIDS told to consider abortion. 1987. *The Plain Dealer.* (20 Feb.).

Women on Medicaid manage to get funding for abortion. 1981. *Nation's Health.* (October).

Would *Roe* go? 1987. *Time.* (21 Sept.):14–15.

FOR FURTHER READING

American Civil Liberties Union. *Parental Notice Laws.* New York: Reproduction Freedom Project, ACLU, 1986.

Boston Women's Health Book Collective. *Our Bodies, Ourselves.* New York: Simon & Schuster, 1984.

Callahan, Daniel. *Abortion: Laws, Choice and Morality.* New York: Macmillan, 1970.

Devereux, George. *A Study of Abortion in Primitive Societies.* New York: Julian Press, 1955.

Emmens, Carol A. *The Abortion Controversy.* New York: Julian Messner, 1987.

Francke, Linda Bird. *The Ambivalence of Abortion.* New York: Random House, 1978.

Imber, Jonathan B. *Abortion and the Private Practice of Medicine.* New Haven: Yale University Press, 1986.

Mohr, James C. *Origins and Evolution of National Policy 1800–1900.* New York: Oxford University Press, 1978.

Nathanson, Bernard N. *Aborting America.* New York: Pinnacle, 1979.

Reagan, Ronald. *Abortion and the Conscience of the Nation.* New York: Thomas Nelson Publishers, 1984.

Rothman, Barbara Katz. *The Tentative Pregnancy.* New York: Viking Penguin, 1986.

Rubin, Eva R. *Abortion, Politics, and the Courts.* Westport, CT: Greenwood Press, 1982.

Shostak, Arthur B., and Gary McLouth. *Men and Abortion.* New York: Praeger, 1984.

Szumski, Bonnie, ed. *Abortion? Opposing Viewpoints.* St. Paul, MN: Greenhaven Press, 1986.

Wilkie, J. C., Dr. and Mrs. *The Handbook of Abortion.* Cincinnati: Hayes Publishing, 1985.

INDEX

Abortifacients, 19, 44, 56
Abortion rates, 72–73
Abortion ratios, 72–73
Abstinence, 77
Adoption, 14, 85, 109, 118–119, 127, 128
Advertising, 38, *39*
Age statistics, 72, 74, 77
Alan Guttmacher Institute (AGI), 70, 76, 96
American Civil Liberties Union (ACLU), 26, 96
American Law Institute, 21
American Medical Association (AMA), 18, 20
Amniotic fluid embolism, 54
Anger, 55
Aspirator, 50
Attitudes about abortion, 81–91; of fathers, 88–90; personal, 85–88, 131–132; of physicians, 90–91, 95; public, 82–85, 91, 131–132

Baptismal names, 16
Beal v. Doe, 65

Birth control, 44, 50, 63, 76–77, 117, 126; history of, 17–28, 74; pill, 44, 74, 76, 117
Blackmun, Justice Harry A., 28, 66
Blacks, 84–85
Blood clots, 54
Blood pressure, *49*
Brown v. Board of Education, 26

California, abortion cases in, 24, 41, 58, 63
Cancer, uterine, 53
Cannula, 51, 52
Catholics and abortion, 20, 84, 96, 97–103, 108, 109, 115, 132; history of, 98–103
Center for Disease Control (CDC), 70
Cervical tearing, 54
China, 71
Civil rights, 26, 30
Clinics, abortion, 59, 60–63, 87, 90; harassment of, *106*, 107–110
Colorado, abortion cases in, 24

Commonwealth v. Bangs, 17
Complications, procedural, 53–54, 56
Comstock Law (1873), 19, 26
Conscience clause, 38
Consent, 34–37, 75; informed, 36–37
Constitutional rights, 30–32, 41, 66, 102, 103, 132. *See also individual amendments*
Costs, 57–68, 79, 83
Counseling, 37, 63, 89, 108, 109

Depression, 54–55
Diaphragm, 17, 117
Dilation, cervical, 46, 50
Dilation and curettage, 51
Dilation and evacuation, 52, 105
Dilators, 50, 51
Doe v. Bolton, 27
Down's Syndrome, 129
Drugs, 19, 22–23, 44

Early abortion procedures, 48–50, 54, 62
Ectopic pregnancy, 56, 100
Education, 83, 84
Eisenstadt v. Baird, 26, 30, 31
Embryo, 43, 44, 48
Emotional effects of abortion, 37, 54–55, 85–90, 111–120
England, abortion cases in, 17
Europe, 17, 71, 73

Facilities, abortion, 60–63
Fathers, attitudes of, 88–90
Fertilization, 17, 20, 43, 44, 46, 48, 126
Fetus, 43, 44, 46, 48, 51; born alive, 53; deformed, 20–24, 82, 88, 98, 119–120, 128–129, 133; first trimester, 44, 46, 48–51, *124;* second trimester, 46, 51–53; viability of, 30, 32, 34, 40, 51, 53, 122–127, 134
Financial aid, 63–68
Finkbine, Sherri, 22–23
First Amendment, 102, 103, 109, 132
First trimester abortions, 32, 44, 46, 48–51, 54, 59, 62, 79, 82, 90, 133
Fourteenth Amendment, 30, 31, 32
Future pregnancies, 56

Georgia, abortion cases in, 27, 28
German measles, 23–24
Gestation, 46, 48, 79
Government subsidies for abortions, 29, 63–68, 83
Griswold v. Connecticut, 26, 30, 31
Guilt, 37, 55

Harassment, abortion clinic, *106,* 107–110
Harris v. McRae, 66
Hartigan v. Zbaraz, 37
History of abortion, 16–28, 57–58, 74–75, 98–103
Hodgson v. Minnesota, 36
Hominization, 99
Hospital abortions, 60, 62, 63
Human Life amendment, 41
Hyde Amendment, 64–68
Hysterectomy, 53
Hysterotomy, 53

Illegal abortions, 13, 57–58, 71, 74, 93; history of, 18–28
Illinois, abortion cases in, 58
Incest, 20, 65, 76, 82, 111, 115–116
Income, 83, 84
Incomplete abortions, 48, 50

Induced abortions, 44, 46
Industry, abortion, 57–68;
  costs, 57–58, 59, 62, 63–68
Infection, 54
Informed consent, 36–37
Instillation, 52–53, 105
Instrumental evacuation, 46,
  50–51
I.U.D., 44, 74

Jane clinic (Chicago), 58
Jews, 84, 96, 97, 133

Lamanaria, 50
Late abortion procedures, 51–
  53, 54, 62
Legal abortions, 13–28, 71, 74–
  75; history of, 16–28; *Roe v.
  Wade* ruling on, 13–16, 27,
  28, 29–42
Life-saving abortions, 65, 66,
  67, 82, 100, 116
Live fetal birth, 53
LMP (last menstrual period),
  48, 50
Lord Ellenborough Act (1803),
  17
Low-income women, 63–68

Maher v. Roe, 65
Marital status, 77–79, 111–113
Massachusetts, abortion cases
  in, 17, *39*
McCorvey, Norma, 13–16
Medicaid, 63–67, 113
Men and abortion, 55, 84, 88–
  90, 132
Menstrual extraction, 48, 50
Minnesota, abortion cases in,
  35–36
Minorities, 21, 85
Minors, abortions for, 29, 34–
  36, 37, 53, 77
Miscarriages, 44, 74
Missouri, abortion cases in, 107

Morals and ethics of abortion,
  121–137; competing, 127–
  131; fetal deformity, 20–24,
  82, 88, 98, 128–129, 133;
  history of, 20–25, 98–103;
  personhood, 123–127; private vs. public, 82–88, 131–
  132; and religion, 98–103,
  107, 108, 132–134; separation of church and state, 98–
  103, 107, 108; sound reasoning, 134–137
Moral Penal Code, 21, 24
Mortality, abortion, 19, 54, 68,
  80, 116–118
Murder, abortion as, 105, 123,
  135; history of, 16, 17, 98–
  103

National Abortion Federation
  (NAF), 63, 107
National Abortion Rights Action League (NARAL), 95
National Conference of Catholic Bishops (NCCB), 102–
  103
National Organization for
  Women (NOW), 95
National Right-to-Life Committee (NRL), 97
Nazi Holocaust, 136
New York, abortion cases in,
  24, 41, 58, 59, 63, 64
Nineteenth century abortion
  laws, 17–19
Ninth Amendment, 31
Non-therapeutic induced abortion, 44, 66
Notification, 37

O'Connor, Justice Sandra, 40
Ohio, abortion cases in, *106*

Pain, 51, 52
Penumbras, 31

Personal attitudes on abortion, 85–88, 131–132
Personhood, 32, 40, 41, 123–127
Physicians, 62, 63, 108; attitudes of, 90–91, 95
Placenta, 44, 46
Planned Parenthood, 26, 70, 91, 96, 119
Politics of abortion, 93–110; pro-choice groups, 81, 93–96, 105, 107, 110; right-to-life groups, 81, 91, 96–98, 103, *104,* 105, *106,* 107–110; separation of church and state, 98–103, 107, 108; tactics used to affect abortion policy, 103–110
Post Abortion Syndrome (PAS), 54–55
Pregnancy tests, 17, 46
Premature infants, 34, 40
Previous abortions, 79
Procedures, abortion, 43–56; complications, 53–54, 56; early, 48–50, 54, 62; effect on future pregnancies, 56; instrumental evacuation, 46, 50–51; late, 51–53, 54, 62
Pro-choice groups, 81, 93–96, 105, 107, 110
Prostaglandin, 50, 52, 53
Protestants, 84, 96, 133–134
Public attitudes on abortion, 82–85, 91, 131–132

Rape, 13, 20, 44, 65, 76, 82, 111, 115–116, 127
Reagan, Ronald, 38, 97
Reasons for abortion, 111–120
Rehnquist, Judge, 38
Religious issues, 20, 83, 84, 96, 97, 112, 115–116, 132–134; separation of church and state, 98–103, 107, 108. *See also specific religions*
Reproductive Freedom Project, 96
Right-to-life groups, 81, 91, 96–98, 128; Catholic, 97–103, 108, 109; tactics, 103, *104,* 105, *106,* 107–110
Right to privacy issue, 29, 30–32, 39, 131–132
Risks, 36, 37, 53–54, 56
Roe v. Wade, 13–16, 27, 28, 29–42, 58, 66, 93, 97, 125; advertising, 38, *39;* conscience clause, 38; consent, 34–37; notification, 37; overturning, 38–40; personhood, 32, 40, 41; right to privacy, 29, 30–32, 39; state regulation, 34, 41; trimesters, 30, 32–34, 40
RU 486, 44, 48, 50, 56
Rural vs. urban abortions, 60, 84

Saline abortions, 52–53
Sanger, Margaret, 91
Second trimester abortions, 30, 32, 34, 46, 51–53, 54, 62, 82, 90, 120, 133
Separation of church and state, 98–103, 107, 108
Slippery slope argument, 134–135
Social class issues, 84–85
Sound reasoning, 134–137
Soviet Union, 71, 73
Spontaneous abortions, 44, 74
State regulation, 34, 41, 66, 67, 75
States' Rights Amendment, 41
Statistics, abortion, 70–80, 111
Sterilization, 77, 117
Suicide, 117–118
Supreme Court rulings, 15, 26–28, 53, 63, 90, 102, 131; on Hyde Amendment, 65–66; *Roe v. Wade,* 16, 27, 28, 29–42, 58, 66, 93, 97, 125

Teenage abortions, 29, 34–36, 37, 53, 77
Terms, abortion, 103–105, 107
Texas, abortion cases in, 13–16, 27
Thalidomide, 22–23
Therapeutic abortions, 20, 44, 99–100
Third trimester abortions, 82, 90
Twelve–week–old fetus, *124*
Twinslayer's Case, 16

Ultrasound, 48, 119
Unplanned pregnancy statistics, 76–77
Urea, 53
Uterine wall perforation, 54

Vacuum abortions, 50–51, 54, 105
Viability of fetus, 30, 32, 34, 40, 51, 53, 122–127, 134
Violence, anti-abortion, *106*, 107–110

White, Justice, 30–31, 38
Women Exploited By Abortion (WEBA), 55
Women's movement, 25–26, 95
Women who obtain abortions, statistics on, 69–80
World War II, 74
Worldwide abortions, 23, 71–72

Zygote, 43, 44, 50

ABOUT THE AUTHOR

Susan Neiburg Terkel grew up in Lansdale, Pennsylvania, and was educated at Cornell University where she studied child development and family relationships. She has published several books for children including *Yoga Is for Me* and *Feeling Safe, Feeling Strong: How to Prevent Sexual Abuse and What to Do If It Happens to You*, which she coauthored with Janice Rench. She lives in Hudson, Ohio, with her husband and three children.

363.46 T
Terkel, Susan Neiburg.
Abortion

Hicksville Public Library
169 Jerusalem Avenue
Hicksville, New York
Telephone Wells 1-1417

Please Do Not Remove
Card From Pocket

HI